Finding the Truth in Story

To Kadence,
True Knowledge is enriching

Tyce Brawell

Finding the Truth in Story

Grimm's Fairy Tales

Volume I

Tyrel Bramwell

GRAIL QUEST BOOKS ✠ BANGOR

Copyright © 2017 by Tyrel Bramwell

Grail Quest Books
71 Broadway #3
Bangor, Maine 04401
www.grailquestbooks.com

"Grail Quest Books" and "Grail Quest Books" and "GQB" logos are trademarks of Grail Quest Books. All rights reserved.

All rights reserved. No portion of this publication may be reproduced, stored in a retrieval system, or transmitted in any form by any means, electronic, mechanical, photocopy, recording, or otherwise, without prior written permission of the publisher.

Scripture quotations are from The ESV® Bible (The Holy Bible, English Standard Version®), copyright © 2001 by Crossway, a publishing ministry of Good News Publishers. Used by permission. All rights reserved.

Cover Image: *King Thrushbeard* by Arthur Rackham, 1909.

Printed in the United States of America.

ISBN-13: 978-1977718785
ISBN-10: 1977718787

For Jonas and Bethany who know the truth that occurred once upon the fullness of time. May you always find the Word of God in the words of man.

Table of Contents

Foreword 10
Author's Note 16
Preface 18
The Frog King 27
The Giant and the Tailor 41
The Little Peasant 53
The Golden Key 76
Sharing Joy and Sorrow 83
The Nail 92
Tom Thumb 98
Tom, Journeyman 116
Sweet Porridge 130
The Young Giant 137
The Elves, Pt I 158
The Elves, Pt II 168
The Elves, Pt III 174
Fair Katrinelje and Pif-Paf-Poltrie 178

The Old Beggar Woman 184
The Jew Among Thorns 188
King Thrushbeard 201
Fitcher's Bird 215
The Robber Bridegroom 230
Old Hildebrand 240
The Singing Bone 253
Maid Maleen 261
The Skillful Huntsman 281
Allerleirauh 297
Cinderella.. 314
Acknowledgements 334

Foreword

I had always felt life first as a story: and if there is a story there is a story teller.

– G.K. Chesterton, *Orthodoxy*

FROM our first words in the morning to our last words at night, our day is full of storytelling. Children share tales of their epic journeys through dream-land at breakfast, adults narrate the plans of their day over coffee, and come dinner time we share the ordinary adventures of everyday life. Yes, we are a storytelling people, hard-wired for creativity by a creative, word-giving God. We create and consume stories, and often for many reasons.

Foreword

At times we read for enjoyment, other times to educate; other times it's a welcomed escape or a book that enlivens the imagination.

Whatever the occasion, reading imparts wisdom, conveys truth, and reveals beauty. Reading enlivens the senses. Finely crafted words and illustrations catch the eyes. Ink and paper fill our nose like a favorite family recipe. Pages flutter between our fingers like a cooling summer breeze. Authors grab our ears like a loving child, begging us to listen to their stories; please, daddy, just one more page. Or, as the Psalmist declares, "How sweet are your words to my taste, sweeter than honey to my mouth!"(Ps.119:103).

Good stories fill us with a sense of wonder, adventure, and longing. We are searching for something within those pages, perhaps it is as simple as reading a well-told story. This in and of itself is a good thing. Though often when we read, our life outside of the pages breaks in and causes to wrestle with questions of existence and importance: wisdom, truth, and beauty; right and wrong, good and evil, suffering and joy, death and life. C.S. Lewis had a word for this inconsolable longing; he called it Joy (see *Surprised by Joy*). It is, as he writes in *Mere*

Christianity, our desire for our true country. For, "if I find in myself a desire which no experience in this world can satisfy, the most probable explanation is that I was made for another world"[1]

Scripture reminds us similarly, the Lord "has put eternity into the heart of man" (Ecc. 3:11). Each of us is like an explorer, looking for answers to our questions, searching for satisfaction to our longing, seeking truth in a world of lies.

It is no wonder, then, that many approach the reading of stories, like Grimm's Fairy Tales, in the same way they read Aesop's Fables, mining the pages for the moral nugget in the story. To be sure, there are important virtues learned from stories. From the story of the Old Beggar Woman we learn that we ought to love our neighbor. From the story of The Skillful Huntsman we learn the dying virtue of chivalry. From the story of The Singing Bone we learn that we truly are our brother's keeper.

But this is only part of what we learn from good stories. As Tyrel Bramwell writes in his commentary on The Old Beggar Woman,

---

[1] C.S. Lewis, *Mere Christianity* (New York: Harper Collins, 2001), 136-137.

Foreword

"When the light of Christianity shines on the stories of man it's easy to see the truth of Scripture in the tales we consume."

We must take the harder, narrow road and guard against mining each story simply for the golden rule, for by doing so, we may lose a story's true treasure in the tailings. We may successfully find the moral of the story and yet still not find the truth in the story. In the language of Holy Scripture, this means that we all too often spend our time looking for the moral, rule, or the Law in any given story, which only leads to pride, despair, and death.

Tyrel Bramwell shows us a better way to read stories, to look for the truth in the story, and with the truth, to find our way and life in the greatest story of all time. Bramwell leads the reader, not up an endless ladder of morality, but rather on a discovery that ends in joy. What Bramwell does so well in this commentary of Grimm's Fairy Tales is lead us to the Truth in the story. And this is what good stories do; they point us to the one Great and True story of Jesus crucified and risen for you. Good stories not only give us a moral to learn (the Law), but give us a glimpse of true joy in the Gospel. Good stories point us to Jesus Crucified who is the Way, the Truth, and the Life; the Great Storyteller who writes himself into his own book and becomes a part of its pages. The Word was made flesh and dwelt among us, John declares (John 1:14). This grand story gives birth to all other stories, and the best stories point us back to this Gospel, the greatest story ever told.

G.K. Chesterton observed a similar fact when it comes to reading good stories.

> My first and last philosophy, that which I believe with unbroken certainty, I learnt in the nursery...There is the lesson of 'Cinderella', which is the same as that of the Magnificat. There is the great lesson of Beauty and the Beast; that a thing must be loved before it is loveable. There is the terrible allegory of the Sleeping Beauty, which tells us how the human creature was blessed with all birthday gifts, yet cursed with death; and how death also may be softened to a sleep.[2]

---

[2] G.K. Chesterton, *Orthodoxy* (Colorado Springs: Waterbrook Press, 2008), 66.

Foreword

Within the pages of this book, you will find Christ's sacrifice in King Thrushbeard's humility; you will find Christ's strength hidden in weakness through characters like Tom Thumb; and you will find Christ's promise of salvation in the most unexpected ways, just as Cinderella did.

Here you will find hope in the midst of despair, joy for times of sorrow, and most important of all, you will find the truth in the story that will lead you to the greatest story of all: Jesus, crucified and risen for you.

Rev. Sam Schuldheisz, 2017
Redeemer Lutheran Church
Huntington Beach, CA

Author's Note

MARGARET Hunt's 1884 translation of the Grimm brothers' German *Kinder- und Hausmärchen* is regarded as the definitive English translation of the tales. I was reading a reproduction of this translation when it occurred to me to slow down and look for the Truth in the stories. For the convenience of today's reader, I have updated the 1884 vocabulary (thee, thou, wither, thither, etc.). Additionally, I have adjusted the layout of each story's text according to modern expectations. The majority of this involved inserting paragraph breaks during dialogue to differentiate between speakers. My goal was to make the Grimm brothers' stories more readily accessible to today's readers who are interested

Author's Note

in finding the Truth of God's Word in the words of these wonderful tales.

Preface

IN the preface to *Orthodoxy*, G.K. Chesterton states that the purpose of the book is "to attempt an explanation, not of whether the Christian Faith can be believed, but of how he personally has come to believe it…. It deals first with all the writer's own solitary and sincere speculations..." He regarded "it as amounting to a convincing creed. But if it is not that it is at least a repeated and surprising coincidence."[3]

In similar fashion I've set out to attempt an explanation of how I personally take in the stories of man. This is the first book of a project I've come to call *Finding the Truth in Story*, an attempt to express my solitary and sincere

---

[3] Chesterton, *Orthodoxy*, xxiii.

speculations on the Christian themes found in various narratives. In this way it's a purely subjective effort. I suspect that it will amount to a convincing creed but if it doesn't, it'll at least reveal a repeated and surprising coincidence.

The Christian faith shapes how I see the world, including humanity's creative efforts. In the words of C.S. Lewis, "I believe in Christianity as I believe that the Sun has risen, not only because I see it, but because by it I see everything else."[4]

As a result, I read the words of men with Christological eyes. It doesn't matter if I'm reading Luther or L'Amour, what Scripture says norms what I read, that is, it sets the standard and defines the boundaries of truth to which everything else must conform. Some writers weave their words better than others. Some express the Christian truth better than others. They do this with various levels of intentionality and obedience to or rebellion against the truth. Eugene Peterson says it like this,

---

[4] C.S. Lewis, *The Weight of Glory*, (New York: Harper Collins Publishers Inc., 2001), 140.

> Words are the means by which the gospel is proclaimed and the stories told. But not all words tell stories or proclaim gospel. All our words have their origin in the Word that was in the beginning with God, the Word that was God, the Word that had made all things (John 1:1-3), but not all words maintain that connection, not all words honor that origin and nurture their relationship with the Source Word, the Creator Word.[5]

The Word he's referring to is the Incarnate Word, Jesus Christ. With that said this project will be an effort to purposefully look for words (stories) that maintain a connection with the Source Word–Jesus–that Christianity has confessed throughout history.

The second century Christian apologist, Justin Martyr, put it this way: "Whatever things were rightly said among all men, are the property of us Christians... For all the writers were able to see realities darkly through the

---

[5] Eugene Peterson, *Under the Unpredictable Plant*, (Grand Rapids: William B. Eerdmans Publishing Company, 1994), 190.

sowing of the implanted word that was in them."[6]

Finding the Truth in Story is an effort to find some of what has been rightly said among men and do what I can in the form of commentary to return the property to its rightful owner. Or put another way, to search out glimpses of truth that point to the Incarnate Word, Jesus Christ, or at the very least call to mind – my mind anyway – a portion of the revealed wisdom of God.

This particular book contains the fruit of my labor with regards to twenty-five of Grimm's fairy tales.

I don't presume to know the minds of the Grimm Brothers. That's irrelevant. My goal is to better see the connectivity between the words of man and the Word of God. It's personal. After all, to quote Lewis again, "Myth is... like manna; it is to each man a different dish and to each the dish he needs."[7]

---

[6] Justin Martyr, "The Second Apology of Justin," in *The Apostolic Fathers with Justin Martyr and Irenaeus*, ed. A. Roberts, J. Donaldson, and A. C. Coxe (Buffalo: Christian Literature Company, 1885), Vol. 1, 193.

[7] C.S. Lewis, "Selected Literary Essays," in *The Quotable Lewis*, ed. Wayne Martindale and Jerry Root (Wheaton: Tyndale House Publishers Inc., 1990), 444.

As a pastor and as a writer, I want to expand my understanding of how to best keep my words connected to God's Word so I can create a responsible subjective apologetic for the faith. It's a personal exercise with consequences that I hope to use as I communicate with others in my various vocations, indeed to serve others in seeing the truth of God's Word.

"As a dream while asleep can touch the depths of our being, could not the literature of wakefulness shower with light and supreme power the landscape of religious concern, and provide the Subjective attestation of Christian truth for which men long?"

John Warwick Montgomery asked that in *Myth, Allegory and Gospel*.[8] He also asked, "If the Faith can be found mirrored in the great literary productions of the time, would this not lead the secular reader to a new appreciation of that 'Faith once delivered to the saints'?"[9]

Great questions, both of them. And I believe the answer is yes. If the Source Word, the Incarnate Word – Jesus Christ – can be seen

---

[8] John Warwick Montgomery, *Myth, Allegory, and Gospel*, (Minneapolis: Bethany Fellowship, Inc., 1974), 20-21.
[9] Ibid., 21.

in the words of man, whether the human author intended the connection or not, nothing less than a thought provoking coincidence will be presented, if not more, that which amounts to a convincing creed.

Joseph Campbell did similar work, however, with the opposite aim. He wrote in the preface to the 1949 edition of *The Hero with a Thousand Faces*, "It is the purpose of the present book to uncover some of the truths disguised for us under the figures of religion and mythology by bringing together a multitude of not-too-difficult examples [myths and folktales] and letting the ancient meaning become apparent of itself."[10]

In other words, his goal was to detach man's words from God's Word. Campbell hoped that comparing the stories of man would unite the people of the world, but as he says, "not in the name of some ecclesiastical or political empire, but in the sense of human mutual understanding."[11]

His work of comparing the similarities of man's stories, has been used to guide the world,

---

[10] Joseph Campbell, *The Hero with a Thousand Faces*, (Novato: New World Library, 2008), xii.
[11] Ibid., xiii.

if by no other way than its influence on creative minds, to see the Word Incarnate as just another one of humanity's words, rather than the original Word that it is. Campbell liked the saying found in the Vedas, "Truth is one, the sages call it by many names."[12]

He used it to say, "Therefore, it is necessary for men to understand, and be able to see, that through various symbols the same redemption is revealed."[13]

I beg to differ. There is one truth. Therefore, it's necessary for the salvation of men that we understand, and be able to see, that all stories (myths, symbols, legends, fairy tales, novels, etc.) allude to, point to, and stem from the reality that redemption comes from knowing the One truth, namely, Christ crucified for the forgiveness of sins.

Campbell searched mankind's stories in an effort to see all words as equal, appearing "out of the activities of the human body and mind."[14] He saw them as "spontaneous productions of the psyche."[15] Christ became just another one of humanity's myths. My goal is contrary to this,

---
[12] Ibid.
[13] Ibid., 335.
[14] Ibid., 1.
[15] Ibid., 2.

to search mankind's stories in an effort to see all words as extending from the One true Word. I believe that the narratives the world produces are veiled reflections of the true Christian narrative and often times unwittingly so. Lewis' words packed my bags for this journey,

> God is more than a god, not less; Christ is more than a Balder, not less. We must not be ashamed of the mythical radiance resting on our theology. We must not be nervous about 'parallels' and 'Pagan Christs': they ought to be there–it would be a stumbling block if they weren't. We must not, in false spirituality, withhold our imaginative welcome.[16]

There is One truth and all people are searching for it. It has been revealed to us in Scripture, which is all about the Word made flesh in the man, Jesus Christ.

> [As] myth transcends thought, Incarnation transcends myth. The heart of Christianity is a myth which is also a fact. The old myth

---

[16] C.S. Lewis, *God in the Dock*, (New York: Inspirational Press, 1970), 344.

> of the Dying God, *without ceasing to be myth* comes down from the heaven of legend and imagination to the earth of history. It *happens*—at a particular date, in a particular place, followed by definable historical consequences. We pass from a Balder or an Osiris, dying nobody knows when or where, to a historical Person crucified (it is all in order) *under Pontius Pilate*. By becoming fact it does not cease to be myth: that is the miracle.[17]

I've started with Grimm's Fairy Tales for three reasons. First, because my daughter had just finished reading them and I wanted to share them with her. I had never read them before and that seemed to be a great travesty. Secondly, these stories are classics that have influenced and informed other creative works in our culture. Finally, I thought a collection of stories would work well as a series of blog posts on my website where the commentary in this book first appeared.

There you have it. It's time to get started. On to the *The Frog-King*!

---

[17] Ibid.

The Frog-King

IN old times when wishing still helped one, there lived a king whose daughters were all beautiful, but the youngest was so beautiful that the sun itself, which has seen so much, was astonished whenever it shone in her face. Close by the King's castle lay a great dark forest, and under an old lime-tree in the forest was a well, and when the day was very warm, the King's child went out into the forest and sat down by the side of the cool fountain, and when she was dull she took a golden ball, and threw it up on high and caught it, and this ball was her favorite plaything.

Now it so happened that on one occasion the princess's golden ball did not fall into the little hand which she was holding up for it, but on to the ground beyond, and rolled straight into the water. The King's daughter followed it with her eyes, but it vanished, and the well was deep, so deep that the bottom could not be seen. On this she began to cry, and cried louder and louder, and could not be comforted. And as she lamented someone said to her, "What ails you, King's daughter? You weep so that even a stone would show pity."

She looked around to the side from where the voice came, and saw a frog stretching forward its thick, ugly head from the water. "Ah! old water-splasher, is it you?" she said; "I am weeping for my golden ball, which has fallen into the well."

"Be quiet, and do not weep," answered the frog, "I can help you, but what will you give me if I bring your plaything up again?"

"Whatever you will have, dear frog," she said. "My clothes, my pearls and jewels, and even the golden crown which I am wearing."

The frog answered, "I do not care for your clothes, your pearls and jewels, or your golden crown, but if you will love me and let me be your companion and play-fellow, and sit by you at your little table, and eat off your little golden plate, and drink out of your little cup, and sleep

The Frog-King

in your little bed—if you will promise me this I will go down below, and bring you your golden ball up again."

"Oh yes," she said, "I promise you all you wish, if you will but bring me my ball back again." She, however, thought, "How the silly frog does talk! He lives in the water with the other frogs, and croaks, and can be no companion to any human being!"

But the frog when he had received this promise, put his head into the water and sank down, and in a short while came swimming up again with the ball in his mouth, and threw it on the grass. The King's daughter was delighted to see her pretty plaything once more, and picked it up, and ran away with it.

"Wait, wait," said the frog. "Take me with you. I can't run as you can." But what did it avail him to scream his croak, croak, after her, as loudly as he could? She did not listen to it, but ran home and soon forgot the poor frog, who was forced to go back into his well again.

The next day when she had seated herself at table with the King and all the courtiers, and was eating from her little golden plate, something came creeping splish splash, splish splash, up the marble staircase, and when it had got to the top, it knocked at the door and cried, "Princess, youngest princess, open the door for me."

She ran to see who was outside, but when she opened the door, there sat the frog in front of it. Then she slammed the door to, in great haste, sat down to dinner again, and was quite frightened.

The King saw plainly that her heart was beating violently, and said, "My child, what are you so afraid of? Is there perchance a giant outside who wants to carry you away?"

"Ah, no," she replied. "It is no giant but a disgusting frog."

"What does a frog want with you?"

"Ah, dear father, yesterday as I was in the forest sitting by the well, playing, my golden ball fell into the water. And because I cried so, the frog brought it out again for me, and because he so insisted, I promised him he should be my companion, but I never thought he would be able to come out of his water! And now he is outside there, and wants to come in to me."

In the meantime it knocked a second time, and cried,

The Frog-King

"Princess! youngest princess!
Open the door for me!
Do you not know what you said to me
Yesterday by the cool waters of the fountain?
Princess, youngest princess!
Open the door for me!"

Then said the King, "That which you have promised you must perform. Go and let him in."

She went and opened the door, and the frog hopped in and followed her, step by step, to her chair. There he sat and cried, "Lift me up beside you."

She delayed, until at last the King commanded her to do it. When the frog was once on the chair he wanted to be on the table, and when he was on the table he said, "Now, push your little golden plate nearer to me that we may eat together."

She did this, but it was easy to see that she did not do it willingly. The frog enjoyed what he ate, but almost every mouthful she took choked her.

At length he said, "I have eaten and am satisfied; now I am tired, carry me into your little room and make your little silken bed ready, and we will both lie down and go to sleep."

The King's daughter began to cry, for she was afraid of the cold frog which she did not like to touch, and which was now to sleep in her pretty, clean little bed. But the King grew angry and said, "He who helped you when you were in trouble ought not afterwards to be despised by you."

So she took hold of the frog with two fingers, carried him upstairs, and put him in a corner. But when she was in bed he crept to her and said, "I am tired, I want to sleep as well as you, lift me up or I will tell your father."

Then she was terribly angry, and took him up and threw him with all her might against the wall. "Now, you will be quiet, odious frog," she said.

But when he fell down he was no frog but a King's son with beautiful kind eyes. He by her father's will was now her dear companion and husband. Then he told her how he had been bewitched by a wicked witch, and how no one could have delivered him from the well but herself, and that tomorrow they would go together into his kingdom. Then they went to sleep, and next morning when the sun awoke

The Frog-King

them, a carriage came driving up with eight white horses, which had white ostrich feathers on their heads, and were harnessed with golden chains, and behind stood the young King's servant Faithful Henry.

Faithful Henry had been so unhappy when his master was changed into a frog, that he had caused three iron bands to be laid around his heart, in case it should burst with grief and sadness. The carriage was to conduct the young King into his Kingdom. Faithful Henry helped them both in, and placed himself behind again, and was full of joy because of this deliverance. And when they had driven a part of the way the King's son heard a cracking behind him as if something had broken. So he turned around and cried, "Henry, the carriage is breaking."

"No, master, it is not the carriage. It is a band from my heart, which was put there in my great pain when you were a frog and imprisoned in the well."

Again and once again while they were on their way something cracked, and each time the King's son thought the carriage was breaking; but it was only the bands which were springing from the heart of faithful Henry because his master was set free and was happy.

* * *

IF Jesus had been a frog and the Church a beautiful princess who gets to live with a handsome prince despite physically abusing him, wanting nothing to do with him, and lying to him, then *The Frog-King* is a story of Christ and His bride, the Church.

In this story we're introduced to a beautiful princess whose face astonished even the sun when it shone on her, the kind of girl who turns heads when she walks by in the mall, but come to find out, when you actually get to know her, is as hideous as can be. At the end of the story she gets into a carriage with the Frog-King to live with him in his kingdom. Which immediately begs the question, why would he want to be with her after the way she treated him? Because she's the Church and he's Christ. If Christ had entered fairyland this is how we might expect the Gospel to read. The Gospel according to Grimm.

Human beauty is said to be found in the embodiment of a person[18]. The princess is the

---

[18] See Roger Scruton's, *Beauty: A Very Short Introduction* for a quick look at the subject.

embodiment of the Church, the beautiful bride of Christ. God's holy Church as He has formed her is indeed beautiful, yet in the dark forest of this fallen world, sin veils her beauty and disfigures her from the inside. Like the princess we who were beautifully made in the image of God, the picture of perfection, dropped the ball and have been behaving poorly in sin ever since. We put our interests before the interests of others. We're fixed on what brings us pleasure. Like the princess we say whatever we have to in order to get what we want. We break promises and flee those in need, leaving them to live in darkness. Like the princess we despise those in our lives who don't measure up to our criteria and only interact with them begrudgingly.

Having dropped her golden ball, the king's daughter laments, weeping like a daughter of Israel (2 Sam. 1:24). It's in the midst of her despair that we're introduced to the frog. Fitting. It's in the midst of our despair that we meet Jesus in his humility, the Word made flesh who came to rescue us from what ails us--sin. In the same way the frog emerges from the waters of the fountain in the forest in order to come to the princess's rescue, his word preceding the revelation of his physical presence.

He comes with his thick, ugly head, disgusting in the eyes of the princess, having "no form or majesty that [she] should look at him, and no beauty that [she] should desire him." (Is. 53:2) He seeks her love and friendly companionship, he insists on it even, wanting to "sit by you at your little table, and eat off your little golden plate, and drink out of your little cup, and sleep in your little bed." She offers to give him whatever he wants, her clothes, pearls and jewels, even her golden crown, but he's not interested in anything less than her love, just like Jesus, who said, "love the Lord your God with all your heart and with all your soul and with all your mind." (Matt. 22:37). The frog isn't interested in provisions nor crowns, resisting, as it were, satanic temptations (Matt. 4:1-11).

But why does he refer to the princess' things as *little*? To a frog they would be huge! Right? Ah, but to God, the infinite, who wants to step into the finite, who wants to live a human life eating, drinking, and sleeping such furnishings would be *little*. Christ lived a *little*, or rather, a humble life. The frog wants a life with the princess, a life that will benefit her as we see at the end of the story, and he's willing to put in the work to get it, from retrieving her ball in the dark depths of the well to physical abuse when the terribly angry princess throws him against a wall with all her might to silence him. The life of Jesus in fairyland. God wanted to live with His people in order to help us, to save us, to bring us to live with Him. And He was willing to put in the work to redeem us; willing to retrieve our sins from the depths of the waters of Baptism—to take them all on himself, to sink into the darkness of death, to bring up that which had fallen, to suffer physical abuse and death when we threw him against the cross with murderous anger in our hearts, using all our might to crucify him in order to silence the Word of God, in order to say with the princess, "Now, you will be quiet, odious frog."

If when we read this fairy tale we fail to see the Christian truth of Baptism in all the fountain and water language, in the "old water-splasher" who swam up like Jesus who came up out of the waters of the Jordan river (Mark 1:10) to restore us to the life we lived before our carelessness under the trees in Eden, if we fail to see the truth of Communion in the frog's desire to be more than just on a chair at the table, but who actually "wanted to be *on* the table" to "eat together" with his bride to be, like Christ who is the very meal served to us when we kneel at the Lord's Table in the Eucharist, if we don't see these truths in the words of this tale, then we'll certainly fail to see the intentionality and willingness of Christ to suffer the cross for our sake in the frog who by "her father's will" became the princess's "dear companion and husband."

How, after everything the princess did to the poor frog, could he say that "no one could have delivered him from the well but herself'? How is it that she treats him with such disdain yet he says she "delivered him from the well"?

Because she did. It's not that she saved him, as we're quick to think. No. She *delivered* him. She delivered him from the waters of the well to the painful surface of the wall. The Church, in all of our sin, delivered Jesus from the waters of Baptism to the wood of the cross. It was his mission all along to suffer the agony we inflicted upon Him. Jesus knew it. "And as Moses lifted up the serpent in the wilderness, so must the Son of Man be lifted up" (John 3:14). He knew it was necessary that He had to suffer the cross in order to undo evil. The frog says the same thing when he croaks the very words that prompted the princess to unleash her wickedness upon him, "lift me up or I will tell your father." It had to be so.

It's the lifting up that kills Christ and delivers the fruit of the cross into our mouths in the distribution of Communion. It's the lifting up of the frog that flings him against the wall and it's the lifting up of the frog that puts him on the table. It's the lifting up of the frog (the humiliation of Jesus) that reveals the glory of the father, for "when he fell down he was no frog but a Kings' son with beautiful kind eyes." It's the lifting up of the frog, of Christ, that enables the princess, the Church, to be brought into His kingdom when He comes for her.

And as everything is set to end happily ever after the Christian reader's mind–my mind anyway–begins to see an eschatological depiction of Christ's return, an end "full of joy because of this deliverance." No more pain and suffering, only the springing of bands from the hearts of the faithful. The "grief and sadness" of the cross of Christ when our Lord was, in the words of the Brothers Grimm, "a frog and imprisoned in the well" is replaced with the freedom and happiness of our Prince as He takes us to live with Him in His Kingdom forever.

The Giant and the Tailor

A certain tailor who was great at boasting but ill at doing, took it into his head to go abroad for a while, and look about the world. As soon as he could manage it, he left his workshop, and wandered on his way, over hill and dale, sometimes here, sometimes there, but ever on and on. Once when he was out he perceived in the blue distance a steep hill, and behind it a tower reaching to the clouds, which rose up out of a wild dark forest. "Thunder and lightning," cried the tailor, "what is that?" and as he was strongly goaded by curiosity, he went boldly towards it. But what made the tailor open his eyes and mouth when he came near it, was to see that the tower had legs, and leapt in one bound over the steep hill, and was now standing as an all-powerful giant before him.

"What do you want here, you tiny fly's leg?" cried the giant, with a voice as if it were thundering on every side.

The tailor whimpered, "I want just to look about and see if I can earn a bit of bread for myself, in this forest."

"If that is what you are after," said the giant, "you may have a place with me."

"If it must be, why not? What wages shall I receive?"

"You shall hear what wages you shall have. Every year three hundred and sixty-five days, and when it is leap-year, one more into the bargain. Does that suit you?"

"All right," replied the tailor, and thought, in his own mind, "a man must cut his coat according to his cloth; I will try to get away as fast as I can."

On this the giant said to him, "Go, little ragamuffin, and fetch me a jug of water."

"Had I not better bring the well itself at once, and the spring too?" asked the boaster, and went with the pitcher to the water.

"What! The well and the spring too," growled the giant in his beard, for he was rather

The Giant and the Tailor

clownish and stupid, and began to be afraid. "That knave is not a fool, he has a wizard in his body. Be on your guard, old Hans, this is no serving-man for you."

When the tailor had brought the water, the giant charged him to go into the forest, and cut a couple of blocks of wood and bring them back.

"Why not the whole forest, at once, with one stroke. The whole forest, young and old, with all that is there, both rough and smooth?" asked the little tailor, and went to cut the wood.

"What! The whole forest, young and old, with all that is there, both rough and smooth, and the well and its spring too," growled the credulous giant in his beard, and was still more terrified. "The knave can do much more than bake apples, and has a wizard in his body. Be on your guard, old Hans, this is no serving-man for you!"

When the tailor had brought the wood, the giant commanded him to shoot two or three wild boars for supper.

"Why not rather a thousand at one shot, and bring them all here?" inquired the ostentatious tailor.

"What!" cried the timid giant in great terror; "Let well alone tonight, and lie down to rest."

The giant was so terribly alarmed that he could not close an eye all night long for thinking what would be the best way to get rid of this accursed sorcerer of a servant. Time brings counsel. Next morning the giant and the tailor went to a marsh, around which stood a number of willow trees. Then the giant said, "Listen, tailor, seat yourself on one of the willow branches, I long of all things to see if you are big enough to bend it down." All at once the tailor was sitting on it, holding his breath, and making himself so heavy that the bough bent down. When, however, he was compelled to draw breath, it hurled him (for unfortunately he had not put his goose in his pocket) so high into the air that he never was seen again, and this to the great delight of the giant. If the tailor has not fallen down again, he must be hovering about in the air.

* * *

WHEN reading *The Giant and the Tailor,* I was immediately struck by the words of Ephesians

2:8-9, "For by grace you have been saved through faith. And this is *not your own doing that no one may boast.*" The tailor, "who was great at boasting but ill at doing," never heard this Gospel truth, yet he illustrates the point brilliantly. He thought he could do for himself, even that which was far beyond his means. He couldn't even handle doing well the normal tasks of a tailor, yet he bragged to the giant that he could do things that the giant could do. In the end the tailor tries to accomplish something that only the giant could achieve, and it, well, proves to be his undoing.

But before we get ahead of ourselves, let's consider the characters in the tale. The Brothers Grimm introduce the Christian to his old sinful self and to God, whom he erroneously tried, in his sin, to escape. The tailor is the picture of what it looks like when we attempt to live life on our own terms. He is me when I reject my vocation in order to serve myself instead of my neighbor, when I exchange what I've been given to do for what I want to do.

As a boaster who shirked his vocational duties, the tailor was dead in trespasses and sins (Eph. 2:1). Paul tells the Christian that it was in these sins that he "once walked, following the course of this world, following the prince of the power of the air." (Eph. 2:2) The tailor, living as an unrepentant sinner, is still walking in the course of this world, he got it in his head to "look about the world. As soon as he could manage it, he left his workshop, and wandered on his way, over hill and dale, sometimes here, sometimes there, but ever on and on."

The way in which he wanders is very telling. It shows that he does, indeed, follow the prince of the power of the air, walking in Satan's footsteps as it were. In the book of Job (1:7) Satan tells God he had been "going to and fro on the earth"... *sometimes here, sometimes there*.. "walking up and down on it"... *over hill and dale*.

A tailor who is "great at boasting but ill at doing" clothes only himself, dresses up his reputation and leaves his neighbor poorly suited to face the world, naked–his sins exposed. In short, he serves himself when he should be serving others. Throughout the entire story we see him doing what he thinks is best for himself. He's looking after *numero uno*, and expresses his self-centered desire to the giant when he says, "I want just to look about and see if I can earn a bit of bread for myself, in this forest." One may think there's nothing wrong with the tailor wishing to earn bread for himself, after all what's wrong with wanting something to eat? And he said he wants to earn it. What a standup guy. It's not like he's looking for a hand out. The problem reveals itself when we consider who the giant represents.

The giant is described as "all powerful" (Luke 1:37; Job 11:7-11) and speaks "with a voice as if it were thundering on every side" (Exodus 19:19). He says to the tailor, "you may have a place with me" (Deut. 33:27; John 12:26; John 14:3). The giant is God!

Sinful man tells God, "I want just to look about and see if *I* can earn a bit of bread for *myself*, in the forest." This statement demonstrates the wretchedness of the tailor. He sees himself as an autonomous being able to provide for himself. We will see by the end of the story that his end is destruction, because his god is his belly (himself), he wants his own glory and that's his shame, his mind is set on earthly things (Phil. 3:19). He tells the Creator of the world, the one who fed Israel in the wilderness, (read Exodus 19 to see some striking similarities between the tailor and

Israel) the one who taught believers to pray "Our Father who art in heaven... give us this day our daily bread," the one who "supplies seed to the sower and bread for food" (2 Cor. 9:10) the one who said "I am the bread of life; whoever comes to me shall not hunger" (John 6:35) that he wants to earn for himself his own bread.

To which the giant, in his graciousness, responds, "If that is what you are after you may have a place with me." That is, God says "If you want bread, I can give you bread."

But the tailor doesn't desire to be with the giant, rather it's something that "must be." He sees his time with God as playing the hand he was dealt, or as he puts it according to his vocation's proverbial wisdom, cutting his coat according to his cloth. Either way he is determined to get away from the giant (God) as fast as he can.

His wish to get away ultimately comes true. Being an unbeliever he is cast out (John 6:36-37), "for such persons do not serve our Lord Christ, but their own appetites, and by smooth talk and flattery they deceive the hearts of the naïve." (Rom. 16:18)

The Giant and the Tailor

We definitely see this run its course in the tale. The giant is described as credulous, clownish, and stupid. The tailor is a smooth talker with all his boasting. But the giant isn't completely fooled–God is never fooled–and discerns that the tailor is a "sorcerer of a servant", a wizard, wicked within, no servant for him.

The brilliance of this tale manifests itself in full force at the end. The tailor claims he can do the things that the all-powerful giant can do. Like a theologian who demands believers be baptized by nothing less than full immersion, he looks at what the giant deems sufficient and says, "But I can do more!" Why only a jug (a sprinkling of water) when I can bring you the entire well and spring too, or like a critical pew-sitter who looks at the simplicity of the Lord's Supper–tiny pieces of plain bread and a sip of basic wine (two or three boars)–and says, "does God really feed us with so little? I would make this meal so much more, much more grand!" (a thousand boars)

The giant perceives the tailor's propensity to think he can do what God can do, and so allows the tailor to, as they say, put his money where his mouth is, to do what man was given to do, but can't do, what God had to do for us on our behalf, that is, live according to the Law. He asks the tailor to get up on a tree. God says to man, I gave you the way in which to live with me, I made you my servant that you could eat with me and live, but you kept saying you didn't need my grace, you kept saying you could do what I can do. Well, okay. I lived under the Law perfectly, obedient even unto death. So go on, get on the cross." The giant says, "I long of all things to see if you are big enough to bend it down."

And wouldn't you know it, sinful man has the audacity to actually think he can do it. We begin to believe our own boastful lies, we actually come to believe we're like God. We believe in ourselves and put our trust in ourselves.

"All at once the tailor was sitting on [the tree], holding his breath, and making himself so heavy that the bough bent down." We even see some godlike progress in what we do. We can make ourselves pretty heavy with all our boasting, and the things we do even seem to be pretty good. We think we can save ourselves by our works, but when we have to breathe–and there will always come a time when we have to breathe–we realize we're not so godlike after all. We exhale and are flung "so high into the air that [we're] never seen again," we're cast away from the presence of God (Ps. 51:11).

Jesus Christ climbed up on the tree and died for us. He breathed for us, He put his trust not in himself, but in his Father and He breathed out His last breath (Luke 23:46). He didn't have to hold His breath to be heavy enough to accomplish the task He was given to do on the tree. He was able to do this because "though he was in the form of God, [he] did not count equality with God a thing to be grasped, but emptied himself, by taking the form of a servant (Phil. 2:6-7).

We're not as big as God. We're not giants. We're sinful man, we can't even breathe on our own or do the tasks of our vocations as well as we ought. When in repentance we recognize this, we see that God knows us and gives us little things to do, things suitable to our vocations, things that serve others as Christ served us. We don't have to hold down trees–be crucified–"for by grace [we] have been saved through faith. And this is not [our] own doing; it is the gift of God, not a result of works, so that no one may boast. For we are his workmanship, created in Christ Jesus for good works, which God prepared beforehand, that we should walk in them." (Eph. 2:8-10)

If only the tailor would have considered his place in life, perhaps then he would have remembered he is a sinner in need of grace and remembered to "put his goose in his pocket."

The Little Peasant

THERE was a certain village wherein no one lived but really rich peasants, and just one poor one, whom they called the little peasant. He had not even so much as a cow, and still less money to buy one, and yet he and his wife did so wish to have one. One day he said to her, "Listen, I have a good thought, there is our gossip the carpenter, he shall make us a wooden calf, and paint it brown, so that it looks like any other, and in time it will certainly get big and be a cow."

The woman also liked the idea, and their gossip the carpenter cut and planed the calf, and painted it as it ought to be, and made it with its head hanging down as if it were eating.

The next morning when the cows were being driven out, the little peasant called the cow-herd and said, "Look, I have a little calf there, but it is still small and still has to be carried."

The cow-herd said, "All right, and took it in his arms and carried it to the pasture, and set it among the grass."

The little calf always remained standing like one which was eating, and the cow-herd said, "It will soon run alone, just look how it eats already!"

At night when he was going to drive the herd home again, he said to the calf, "If you can stand there and eat your fill, you can also go on your four legs; I don't care to drag you home again in my arms."

But the little peasant stood at his door, and waited for his little calf, and when the cow-herd drove the cows through the village, and the calf was missing, he inquired where it was. The cow-herd answered, "It is still standing out there eating. It would not stop and come with us."

But the little peasant said, "Oh, but I must have my beast back again."

The Little Peasant

Then they went back to the meadow together, but someone had stolen the calf, and it was gone.

The cow-herd said, "It must have run away."

The peasant, however, said, "Don't tell me that," and led the cow-herd before the mayor, who for his carelessness condemned him to give the peasant a cow for the calf which had run away.

And now the little peasant and his wife had the cow for which they had so long wished, and they were heartily glad, but they had no food for it, and could give it nothing to eat, so it soon had to be killed. They salted the flesh, and the peasant went into the town and wanted to sell the skin there, so that he might buy a new calf with the proceeds. On the way he passed by a mill, and there sat a raven with broken wings, and out of pity he took him and wrapped him in the skin. As, however, the weather grew so bad and there was a storm of rain and wind, he could go no farther, and turned back to the mill and begged for shelter.

The miller's wife was alone in the house, and said to the peasant, "Lay yourself on the straw there," and gave him a slice of bread with cheese on it. The peasant ate it, and lay down with his skin beside him, and the woman thought, "He is tired and has gone to sleep."

In the meantime came the parson; the miller's wife received him well, and said, "My husband is out, so we will have a feast."

The peasant listened, and when he heard about feasting he was vexed that he had been forced to make do with a slice of bread with cheese on it. Then the woman served up four different things, roast meat, salad, cakes, and wine.

Just as they were about to sit down and eat, there was a knocking outside. The woman said, "Oh, heavens! It is my husband!" She quickly hid the roast meat inside the tiled stove, the wine under the pillow, the salad on the bed, the cakes under it, and the parson in the cupboard in the entrance. Then she opened the door for her husband, and said, "Thank heaven, you are back again! There is such a storm, it looks as if the world were coming to an end."

The miller saw the peasant lying on the straw, and asked, "What is that fellow doing there?"

"Ah," said the wife, "the poor knave came in the storm and rain, and begged for shelter, so I gave him a bit of bread and cheese, and showed him where the straw was."

The man said, "I have no objection, but be quick and get me something to eat."

The woman said, "But I have nothing but bread and cheese."

"I am contented with anything," replied the husband, "so far as I am concerned, bread and cheese will do," and looked at the peasant and said, "Come and eat some more with me."

The peasant did not require to be invited twice, but got up and ate.

After this the miller saw the skin in which the raven was, lying on the ground, and asked, "What have you there?"

The peasant answered, "I have a soothsayer inside it."

"Can he foretell anything to me?" said the miller.

"Why not?" answered the peasant, "but he only says four things, and the fifth he keeps to himself."

The miller was curious, and said, "Let him foretell something for once."

Then the peasant pinched the raven's head, so that he croaked and made a noise like krr, krr.

The miller said, "What did he say?"

The peasant answered, "In the first place, he says that there is some wine hidden under the pillow."

"Bless me!" cried the miller, and went there and found the wine. "Now go on," he said.

The peasant made the raven croak again, and said, "In the second place, he says that there is some roast meat in the tiled stove."

"Upon my word!" cried the miller, and went there, and found the roast meat.

The peasant made the raven prophesy still more, and said, "Thirdly, he says that there is some salad on the bed."

"That would be a fine thing!" cried the miller, and went there and found the salad.

At last the peasant pinched the raven once more till he croaked, and said, "Fourthly, he says that there are some cakes under the bed."

"That would be a fine thing!" cried the miller, and looked there, and found the cakes.

And now the two sat down at the table together, but the miller's wife was frightened to death, and went to bed and took all the keys with her. The miller would have liked much to know the fifth, but the little peasant said,

The Little Peasant

"First, we will quickly eat the four things, for the fifth is something bad."

So they ate, and after that they bargained how much the miller was to give for the fifth prophesy, until they agreed on three hundred thalers. Then the peasant once more pinched the raven's head till he croaked loudly.

The miller asked, "What did he say?"

The peasant replied, "He says that the Devil is hiding outside there in the cupboard in the entrance."

The miller said, "The Devil must go out," and opened the house door; then the woman was forced to give up the keys, and the peasant unlocked the cupboard. The parson ran out as fast as he could, and the miller said, "It was true; I saw the black rascal with my own eyes."

The peasant, however, made off next morning by daybreak with the three hundred thalers.

At home the small peasant gradually launched out; he built a beautiful house, and the peasants said, "The small peasant has certainly been to the place where golden snow falls, and people carry the gold home in shovels."

Then the small peasant was brought before the Mayor, and bidden to say from where his wealth came. He answered, "I sold my cow's skin in the town, for three hundred thalers."

When the peasants heard that, they too wished to enjoy this great profit, and ran home, killed all their cows, and stripped off their skins in order to sell them in the town to the greatest advantage.

The Mayor, however, said, "But my servant must go first."

When she came to the merchant in the town, he did not give her more than two thalers for a skin, and when the others came, he did not give them so much, and said, "What can I do with all these skins?"

Then the peasants were vexed that the small peasant should have therefore overreached them, wanted to take vengeance on him, and accused him of this treachery before the Mayor.

The innocent little peasant was unanimously sentenced to death, and was to be rolled into the water, in a barrel pierced full of holes. He was led forth, and a priest was brought who was to say a mass for his soul. The others were all obliged to retire to a distance, and when the peasant looked at the priest, he recognized the man who had been with the miller's wife. He said to him, "I set you free from the cupboard, set me free from the barrel."

At this same moment up came, with a flock of sheep, the very shepherd who as the peasant knew had long been wishing to be Mayor, so he cried with all his might, "No, I will not do it; if the whole world insists on it, I will not do it!"

The shepherd hearing that, came up to him, and asked, "What are you about? What is it that you will not do?"

The peasant said, "They want to make me Mayor, if I will but put myself in the barrel, but I will not do it."

The shepherd said, "If nothing more than that is needful in order to be Mayor, I would get into the barrel at once."

The peasant said, "If you will get in, you will be Mayor."

The shepherd was willing, and got in, and the peasant shut the top down on him; then he took the shepherd's flock for himself, and drove it away.

The parson went to the crowd, and declared that the mass had been said. Then they came and rolled the barrel towards the water.

When the barrel began to roll, the shepherd cried, "I am quite willing to be Mayor."

They believed no otherwise than that it was the peasant who was saying this, and answered, "That is what we intend, but first you shall look about yourself a little down below there," and they rolled the barrel down into the water.

After that the peasants went home, and as they were entering the village, the small peasant also came quietly in, driving a flock of sheep and looking quite contented.

Then the peasants were astonished, and said, "Peasant, where do you come from? Have you come out of the water?"

"Yes, truly," replied the peasant, "I sank deep, deep down, until at last I got to the bottom; I pushed the bottom out of the barrel, and crept out, and there were pretty meadows on which a number of lambs were feeding, and from there I brought this flock away with me."

The peasants said, "Are there any more there?"

"Oh, yes," he said, "more than I could do anything with."

Then the peasants made up their minds that they too would fetch some sheep for

The Little Peasant

themselves, a flock apiece, but the Mayor said, "I come first."

So they went to the water together, and just then there were some of the small fleecy clouds in the blue sky, which are called little lambs, and they were reflected in the water, whereupon the peasants cried, "We already see the sheep down below!"

The Mayor pressed forward and said, "I will go down first, and look about me, and if things promise well I'll call you." So he jumped in; splash! went the water; he made a sound as if he were calling them, and the whole crowd plunged in after him as one man.

Then the entire village was dead, and the small peasant, as sole heir, became a rich man.

* * *

TWO marvelous truths seep through the pores of this story. First, this tale is a wonderfully creative expression of the Great Reversal, the reality that though we're guilty of breaking God's Law we get Christ's reward and though He's innocent, having never broken the Law, He suffered the corporal punishment we deserve.

The innocent punished, the guilty set free (Is. 53:5).

This theme is woven throughout the story from beginning to end. In the first sentence the contrast between the guilty multitude and the innocent individual is firmly established in terms of rich and poor: "There was a certain village wherein no one lived but really rich peasants, and just one poor one, whom they called the little peasant." The story's final sentence, a summary sentence, brings the reader back to the main point, the Great Reversal: "Then the entire village was dead, and the small [poor] peasant, as sole heir, became a rich man."

The second truth, relating to the first, is that by having faith in Christ we become little Christs–Christians–still sinners, yes, but sainted sinners, both saints and sinners at the same time, *simil justus et peccator.*

Throughout the narrative we gain insight into the behavior of our two main characters, the little peasant and everyone else, which gives depth to the magnitude of the reversal and reveals that the *little* peasant is a unique Christ figure, a *little* one who lives in "a certain village wherein no one lived but really rich peasants."

The Little Peasant

The little peasant is not a representation of Jesus like the Frog is in *The Frog-King*, but is rather a depiction of the Christian, a little Christ. He is you or me – a sinful being – who is, through the work of Jesus, at the same time innocent, one who is simultaneously in need of Christ's Great Reversal gift and the enfleshed means by which it's shared with the other sinners in his life. It's a great privilege to be a little Christ and being one, as we shall see, has a real impact on the lives of those around us.

At this point the critical reader, especially if he is a Christian with skin in the game, may feel compelled to argue that the actions of the little peasant (e.g. how he deceives the miller with the raven and tricks the shepherd to take his place in the barrel of death) hardly represent Christian behavior. However, this same critical reader, if he is indeed a Christian, may want to pause for a moment and consider just how sinful he truly is, and yet he himself is, despite his sinfulness, a little Christ to those in his life. If this is not enough to allow the little peasant to stand as a picture of the Christian, then perhaps it will help to keep in mind that we're dealing with a fairy tale wherein certain facts are given by the storytellers.

Our protagonist remains untainted when we fasten our view of his actions to the authors' declaration that when "the peasants were vexed that the small peasant should have therefore overreached them, [they] wanted to take vengeance on him, and accused him of this treachery before the Mayor. The *innocent* little peasant was unanimously sentenced to death..."

We may wish to find fault in the little peasant's behavior, however, according to the Brothers' Grimm, to do so would be to bear false witness against their poor *innocent* peasant. We're to read his actions as being without sin. Like Christ before the Sanhedrin (Matt. 26:57-67), he was innocent and yet sentenced to death. Any other view of the little peasant numbers the reader among the rich peasants who would have the small peasant "rolled into the water, in a barrel pierced full of holes."

Though we may not understand exactly how it can be (just as it is hard to see how I, a poor miserable sinner, can be a little Christ in real life), but by trusting the authority of the authors, we're free to see the peasant as a picture of what it looks like in fairyland to be a "sheep in the midst of wolves,... wise as serpents and innocent as doves" (Matt. 10:16), to see how the Great Reversal declares us innocent.

But before the peasant is sentenced to death, the richness of the Great Reversal is further revealed. His gossip, the carpenter, equips him with what he needs to ultimately become a truly rich heir. When I read this I was reminded of something Richard Lischer wrote in his book *Open Secrets:*

> "The word *gossip* originally implied a spiritual relationship. A gossip was a sponsor at a baptism, one who spoke on behalf of the child and who would provide spiritual guidance to the child as it grew in years. A gossip was your godmother or godfather. Gossiping was speech within the community of the baptized."[19]

A Christian — the little peasant — is served by Christ through the gossiping carpenter. It is not hard to make the connection between the

---

[19] Richard Lischer, *Open Secrets* (New York: Broadway Books, 2001), 95.

carpenter and Christ (Mark 6:3), especially one whose business is "speech within the community of the baptized," that is, the proclamation of the Word! And wouldn't you know it, the ultimate result of receiving the Carpenter's work is nothing less than a rich life, not without suffering, but a rich life indeed, one that is set in motion by the work of a gossip (baptismal speech), through the midst of water, and that is strengthened by a feast distributed by the miller, a man who makes flour for bread.

But perhaps you missed the sacramental undertone of the mill scene. After the gossip-carpenter blesses him, the little peasant finds himself seeking shelter at a mill. The way the miller's wife interacts with him and the parson is reminiscent of both the beginning of the story of Lazarus and the Rich Man (Luke 16:19-21), and a parable told by Jesus to people like ourselves who have a tendency to treat others with contempt while trusting in our own righteousness (Luke 18:9-14).

In the parable two men, a righteous Pharisee (the parson) and a sinful tax collector (the little peasant) go up to the temple (the mill) to pray (seek shelter from the storm). The Lazarus-like peasant has to lay on straw and eat

The Little Peasant

only a slice of bread with cheese while the parson is received with a feast of "roast meat, salad, cakes and wine." Our story reveals just "who went down to his house justified" (Luke 18:14) by the wife's husband and who, in the words of the miller, is "the Devil."

"For everyone who exalts himself will be humbled, but the one who humbles himself will be exalted" (Luke 18:14).

That the blessed peasant has been justified is recognized by the other peasants who conclude that he "has certainly been to the place where golden snow falls, and people carry the gold home in shovels," a fairyland description of heaven to be sure.

And indeed he had! At least in the sense that he had received a foretaste of heaven. Having entered the mill (where flour for bread is ground) through the wet and windy (Spirit filled?) waters of a storm (think Baptism) he found shelter and a feast, which he ate in haste (like the Passover, which Jesus celebrated in the upper room where He instituted the Lord's Supper: Ex. 12:11, Luke 22:11-13) with the miller Himself after receiving only simple bread from the miller's wife.

In this scene the little peasant is being served by the miller in a way that again, like the carpenter, calls to mind how Christians are served by Christ. In Communion we receive a simple piece of bread, but what we eat leads to a feast (Rev. 19:9)! The bread—the very body of Christ—is the foretaste of the feast to come for us little Christs. This whole sacramental meal is further highlighted by the words of the miller when the peasant pinches the raven's head.

The first time, immediately before finding the wine, the miller says, "Bless me!" A simplified version of what Paul wrote about the Eucharistic wine when he penned, "The cup of blessing that we bless, is it not a participation in the blood of Christ?" (1 Cor.10:16)

"Upon my word!" the miller says as the roast meat is revealed. The flesh, if you will, upon which he and the little peasant eventually dine inspires thoughts of the incarnation of Jesus, namely that it's His very flesh we're given to eat in the Lord's Supper.

Sadly, the world doesn't understand what occurs in the sacramental meal, how it delivers to the Christian his treasure, a truth that the Grimm brothers cleverly convey when the village peasants misunderstand how the little peasant came into "three hundred thalers." This prompts them to go through the same outward motions he did, killing their cows and going into town to sell the skins, but to no avail. We could say that what was a blessing to the little peasant is a curse to the other peasants. Consequently, they are vexed (1 Pet. 2:7-8).

After the little peasant is sentenced to die we come across another example of the Christian being served by Christ, lest in the midst of our suffering we forget that our Lord knows our pain firsthand and is with us to the very end (Gal 2:20; Heb. 3:14; 13:5-6; John 15:18). This time it's not Jesus as the carpenter or the miller, but rather Jesus as He describes Himself in John 10:11-18, "the [good] shepherd who was willing" to take the little peasant's place in the barrel. The Christian is served by Christ through the Great Reversal.

The shepherd takes the place of the little peasant and the little peasant "took the shepherd's flock for himself, and drove it away." The Grimm brothers were even mindful of the fact that the Great Reversal was carried out by the hands of sinners. The Innocent is not only crucified in the place of the guilty, but by the guilty. In other words, "the peasant shut the top [of the barrel] down on [the shepherd]."

I was the one who killed my Lord!

That no one takes Jesus' life from Him, but that He lays it down of His own accord (John 10:18) comes through in the story "when the barrel began to roll [toward the water and] the shepherd cried, 'I am quite willing to be Mayor.'" Indeed, Mayor of mayors (Rev. 19:16)!

True to God's Word (Matt. 27:27-31) the Brothers Grimm tell us that those charged with carrying out the death sentence "believed no otherwise than that it was" the peasant they were killing and they mocked the man in the barrel, that is on the cross, saying that they intended to make him Mayor—"Hail, King of the Jews!"—"and they rolled him into the water," or in the words of Matthew 27:31, "and led him away to crucify him."

God's Word teaches that, "I have been crucified with Christ; and it is no longer I who live, but Christ lives in me; and the life which I now live in the flesh I live by faith in the Son of God, who loved me and gave Himself up for me" (Gal. 2:20). This is made perfectly clear in the story's conclusion. The rich peasants, in their astonishment, ask the little peasant, "where do you come from? Have you come out of the water?" To which he replies, with a perfect and confident understanding of Baptism, "Yes, truly, I sank deep, deep down, until at last I got to the bottom; I pushed the bottom out of the barrel, and crept out, and there were pretty meadows on which a number of lambs were feeding, and from there I brought this flock away with me" (Rom. 6:3-11).

The village peasants again want the blessings revealed to them through the life of the little peasant, and they push forward with sinful clumsiness. Interestingly enough, we don't see their demise–not at all–we see their salvation, their baptism. It can be argued that the ultimate message conveyed in this story is that if you're not like the little peasant, you'll die. This is true. Those who are not little Christs will die eternally. But that is not the full measure of the message. The story doesn't end with the Law, but with the Gospel. The death of the peasants is not as dark as one might think. I understand the end of *The Little Peasant* to say, be like the little peasant and die. Die to sin, die to self. This is what the village peasants do. They see the life of the little peasant and follow in his footsteps. He leads them to Christ!

They look down into the (baptismal) waters, and what do they see but the wonders of the heavens above. There is obvious misunderstanding at play on the human level, but that doesn't nullify the mysterious divine truth that's evident as well. They drown in pursuit of the heavenly treasures; everything they did was in reaction to seeing what the little peasant had. The life of the Christian is appealing; people want our heavenly treasure– Christ crucified for the forgiveness of sins. Not everyone believes, but those who do, like "the whole crowd [that] plunged in after" the Mayor "as one man," are baptized and become Christians.

This fairy tale ends, well... happily ever after. Not just for the little peasant, but for everyone in the story, for they were all baptized, everyone died in the waters of Baptism as one man. "For by one Spirit we were all baptized into one body," (1 Cor. 12:13) the body of Christ (Rom. 6:4), the shepherd who died willingly to become the Mayor. Yes, the rich lost everything, even their lives while the poor gained it all, but Jesus "came not to call the righteous, but sinners" (Mark 2:17), the peasants. The truth of the matter is, Jesus called the little peasant and He called all the rest.

Why, then is the little peasant said to be the sole heir? Consider the words of 1 Peter 1:3-4, "[Jesus'] divine power has granted to us all things that pertain to life and godliness, through the knowledge of Him who called us to His own glory and excellence, by which He has granted to us His precious and very great promises, so that through them you may become partakers of the divine nature, having escaped from the corruption that is in the world because of sinful desire." The little peasant, as he led the other peasants to the waters of Christian baptism, is positioned as inspiration to do the same for anyone who may read his story.

The Golden Key

IN the winter time, when deep snow lay on the ground, a poor boy was forced to go out on a sledge to fetch wood. When he had gathered it together, and packed it, he wished, as he was so frozen with cold, not to go home at once, but to light a fire and warm himself a little. So he scraped away the snow, and as he was clearing the ground, he found a tiny, gold key. As a result, he thought that where the key was, the lock must be also, and dug in the ground and found an iron chest.

"If the key does but fit it!" he thought; "no doubt there are precious things in that little box."

He searched, but no keyhole was there. At last he discovered one, but so small that it was

The Golden Key

hardly visible. He tried it, and the key fit it exactly. Then he turned it once around, and now we must wait until he has quite unlocked it and opened the lid, and then we shall learn what wonderful things were lying in that box.

* * *

THIS story takes place "in the winter time." Of course it does. If you think about the seasons in terms of life and death, winter is a time where death seems to make a stand in an effort to reign over us. It's a bleak season, void of the life that had blossomed in the spring and filled the days of summer. It's a time where the vibrant colors of the previous seasons, having peaked in the fall, are siphoned from the landscape. The light of day is shorter and the darkness of night lasts longer. Add in a "deep snow [that] lay on the ground" and we have the perfect setting for expressing the gift we've been given in Jesus.

Upon this cold, dark, snow-covered backdrop of winter "a poor boy was forced," by the conditions of the weather and the apparent fact that his supply of wood was depleted "to go out on a sledge to fetch wood." Perhaps today's readers, living in homes heated by furnaces controlled by the push of a button or the turn of a knob, miss the gravity of the situation presented in this tale's first sentence. The ice giant, Winter, is poised to kill a poor boy who, at that very moment, was without the only thing capable of repelling the giant's frigid bite, fire. No wood, no fire. No fire and the cold of winter wins the day, which means death for the poor boy. He's "so frozen with cold" that he can't even make it back home with the wood before starting a fire. He has to warm himself first. This is a dire situation indeed. Death is at the door. This is a survival story.

In this predicament, while on a journey to search for the necessity of life in the midst of a deathly winter, the poor boy finds "a tiny, gold key." And if there is a key there must be a lock as well. Naturally.

If, when the facts of Jesus' life are presented to a person and he realizes that this man, who was born in Bethlehem (a birth celebrated in the winter), actually lived and is recognized throughout history as a teacher--a key to unlock truth--then he must come to terms with the reality that what Jesus taught must either be true or false. And then if, upon a closer look the person discovers, well, yes, what He taught is most certainly true, then Jesus is not just a key like other keys, no, He's the Golden Key and what He unlocks is described in our tale as "an iron chest," a "little box" wherein "no doubt there are precious things."

Now let us consider this box for a moment. It has precious things inside and at the end of the story the boy is in the midst of unlocking it, leaving us in anticipation, waiting to "learn what wonderful things were lying in that box."

The box is the will of God for all people and inside it awaits heaven. What's more, this box full of wonderful things, God's will, had been out amidst the "deep snow" of death that lay about us the whole time.

How many people don't even consider the will of God to be a reality? How many people don't know or don't care about the precious things of heaven: forgiveness, salvation, and life everlasting? It's not a concern for people, they don't even know the little box is out there because it's been hidden by the dark season of sin that we live in. But it's there. Right under our feet, and it has been the whole time.

When the boy inspected the little box, he didn't immediately find a keyhole. When we look at the will of our Father in heaven, we don't immediately see a way to unlock heaven. We see that we can't live by God's good and holy Law. We appear to be locked out, unable to access the "precious things" our Lord wants us to have (Matt. 7:7-11). We live in a world full of keys--teachers: Buddha, Muhammed, Ellen DeGeneres--that claim to have the answer to life, the way to health, wealth, and happiness, the means to achieve immortality and escape pain forever, or perhaps to simply disregard eternity as a concern altogether. There is an abundance of keys for us to choose from, and so as the boy inspects the box we might expect him to find one of two things: either a multitude of keyholes, one for each key, allowing him to simply use the one that best suits his liking or is easily accessible to him at the time; or the box will have one keyhole that will only work with one particular key, as is usually the case with chests.

"At last he discovered" a keyhole. One keyhole "so small that is was hardly visible."

Why would the keyhole be small? To emphasize the point being made. There's only one key that unlocks God's will, one key that gains for us access to the "precious things" of heaven. And in a world full of keys, it's a tiny one, far too often overlooked and taken for granted, dismissed and rejected. Of course, the hole would be small, the boy found a tiny key. If he had been accustomed to little keys perhaps he would have detected the hole quicker. When it comes to keys, tiny ones are not the norm.

The tiny golden key is Jesus (John 14:6-7). But Jesus is more than just the key. The value of a key is found in the lock that it opens. "Where the key was, the lock must be also." Jesus is both the tiny key and the small keyhole (John 10:9). This story draws the reader to what Jesus teaches in Matthew 7:13-14,

> "Enter by the narrow gate. For the gate is wide and the way is easy that leads to destruction, and those who enter by it are many. For the gate is narrow and the way is hard that leads to life, and those who find it are few."

Jesus fulfilled the will of the Father perfectly; He's the one precious key that fit the lock of the Law on the chest of God's will, opening up to us the most holy of holy places, heaven (Eph.

2:18; Heb. 10:19-20), and giving us access to His gifts.

With this in mind, the end of the story is a delightful picture of the post-resurrection now-but-not-yet reality in which the Church resides. Jesus lived His life, "he turned it once around," (Heb. 9:26-27) giving us the "precious things" of God: forgiveness, salvation, and eternal life. We have them now! They are ours today. "And now we must wait until he has quite unlocked it and opened the lid, and then we shall learn what wonderful things were lying in that box" (Heb. 9:28). Until Christ returns, ours is a life of anticipation. We wait for our Lord to come again so that we will know fully the wonderful things that are in the box (Rom. 8:18). Or as St. Paul put it, "Now I know in part; then I shall know fully" (1 Cor. 13:12).

Sharing Joy and Sorrow

THERE was once a tailor, who was a quarrelsome fellow, and his wife, who was good, industrious, and pious, never could please him. Whatever she did, he was not satisfied, but grumbled and scolded, and knocked her about and beat her. As the authorities at last heard of it, they had him summoned, and put in prison in order to make him better. He was kept for a while on bread and water, and then set free again. He was forced, however, to promise not to beat his wife any more, but to live with her in peace, and share joy and sorrow with her, as married people ought to do.

All went on well for a time, but then he fell into his old ways, and was surly and quarrelsome. And because he dared not beat her, he would seize her by the hair and tear it out. The woman escaped from him, and sprang out into the yard, but he ran after her with his yard-measure and scissors, and chased her about, and threw the yard-measure and scissors at her, and whatever else came his way. When he hit her he laughed, and when he missed her, he stormed and swore. This went on so long that the neighbors came to the wife's assistance. The tailor was again summoned before the magistrates, and reminded of his promise.

"Dear gentlemen," he said, "I have kept my word, I have not beaten her, but have shared joy and sorrow with her."

"How can that be," said the judge, "when she continually brings such heavy complaints against you?"

"I have not beaten her, but just because she looked so strange I wanted to comb her hair with my hand; she, however, got away from me, and left me quite spitefully. Then I hurried after her, and in order to bring her back to her duty, I threw at her as a well-meant admonition whatever came readily to hand. I have shared joy and sorrow with her also, for whenever I hit her I was full of joy, and she of sorrow, and if I missed her, then she was joyful, and I sorry."

The judges were not satisfied with this answer, but gave him the reward he deserved.

* * *

THIS is not a story for our time. We, in our postmodernity, cannot begin to get out of it what its original audience would have. How can we? It speaks in terms of certainty. We know no certainty. As readers today take in the story of the quarrelsome tailor and his battered wife, some may experience varying levels of sympathy or empathy toward the woman, or perhaps even the abusive husband, but that's about it. Some may find amusement in the man's failed attempt at cleverness, and I suspect those who have knowledge of divorce hearings may even recognize just how prevalent his faulty logic is in our world. Perhaps they would testify that there's a good chance he wasn't being clever at all, that he was probably—frustratingly—simpleminded but sincere. If that's the case, then he might find some supporters who wish to champion his position among the twenty-first century audience.

But that's the end of the story's value for today's readers, for the rest of it hangs on words having definitions, on authority, on what "people ought to do," and on truth that is knowable.

Consider the use of the adjective *good*. In the real world we no longer know what good means, words and their meanings are relative. No one is to cast judgment on someone else, say a wife, to determine if she is *good*. In light of the given information, that the tailor's wife "never could please" her husband, a person might say she, therefore, must not have been very good (depending on how we understand good), and if we cannot determine whether or not she was good, how are we to know anything about her being industrious and pious?

Had we been exposed to this narrative by our grandmother, say, over a cup of coffee, we'd have no problem believing it to be about a real life event, perhaps something she saw on the evening news. There is nothing that prompts us to locate this story in fairyland, that is, except for the acknowledgement of authority and life ordered according to the discernable ought. If such things exist today, it must only be in fairyland. While we do still listen to the authorities, to varying degrees, it is always with a sense of subjectivity: I won't murder because the consequence is prison and I'd probably get caught, but I will drive ten miles over the speed limit because I could pay the ticket and the odds of getting pulled over seem low. As a society we would never be so presumptuous as to say there is a way people *ought* to behave.

We understand that the fairyland authorities are brought in merely because we assume, like in our society, that there are laws against hurting people. We expect the authorities to see to the woman's safety, but on what grounds? Where does their jurisdiction come from? The redefining of marriage by the Supreme Court in America[20] reveals the sad truth that we don't know the foundation of our laws, of law in general, a problem, by the way that's similar and indeed connected to a failure to recognize that all words extend from the source Word. We've forgotten where government gets its authority–God (Rom. 13:1).

The brothers Grimm, however, show us that the fairyland courts are not detached from

---

[20] Obergefell v. Hodges, 576 U.S. ___ (2015)

God's will. Their words and laws rest on God's Word. It's the assumption of how "married people ought to" live that is telling. They are to live in peace and share joy and sorrow (Eph. 5:22-33). Husband and wife share everything. They are, after all, one flesh (Gen. 2:24; Matt. 19:4-6; Eph. 5:31). Based on the behavior of the judges in this tale, I imagine the citizens of fairyland find it far easier to live according to Romans 13 than do American Christians today who are trying to discern just what Acts 5:29 looks like in our setting.

Interestingly enough, nowhere in this story do we read that the woman went to the authorities on her own behalf. The first time her husband is brought before the magistrates, we're told that "the authorities at last heard of" her being beaten. It's not at all implied that she went to them and reported her husband. It took a while for them to hear of what was happening. The second time the magistrates get involved it's because the abuse went on so long that the neighbors finally came to her assistance. This reflects the reality of the situation. How many wives live with this kind of treatment for years in the hope that their husband will change? You don't have to be a Christian to want to love your spouse and hope he or she will change. This woman lived as real battered wives do. She also lived as real Christian wives do. This poor woman did everything in her power to endure, not only as a wife, but from what we've gathered from our journey through fairyland so far, as a Christian wife. It's pure speculation to be sure, but if she was a Christian wouldn't her behavior be in keeping with what St. Paul says in 1 Corinthians 7:14-16:

> For the unbelieving husband is made holy because of his wife, and the unbelieving wife is made holy because of her husband… God has called you to peace. For how do you know, wife, whether you will save your husband? Or how do you know, husband, whether you will save your wife?

Perhaps her endurance was because of her faith and she hoped to save her husband. Not because he deserved it, but because she loved him, because of self-sacrificing grace, because she was a Christian and wanted to lead him to Christ (see the chapter on The Little Peasant). He didn't live as a Christian husband, and if not a Christian husband, then not a Christian. Our faith permeates all aspects of our lives. It shapes who we are in all our vocations, our behavior providing evidence that we have faith (James 2:14-17). He certainly didn't love his wife as Christ loved the Church (Eph. 5:25), he didn't love her as his own body (Eph. 5:28), instead he defied God's Word that says, "He who loves his wife loves himself. For no one ever hated his own flesh, but nourishes and cherishes it, just as Christ does the church" (Eph. 5:28-29) and "Husbands, love your wives, and do not be harsh with them" (Col. 3:19).

The abusive husband tried to hypocritically justify his sinful behavior, expressing to the authorities that he wanted to "bring [his wife] back to her duty," while he himself demonstrated the rejection of his own. "The judges were not satisfied with his answer, but gave him the reward he deserved." The authors of the story assume their readers know what the husband deserved. They assume a knowable truth, but how are we to know such a thing in our world of uncertainty? We live in a time where truth is wrongly perceived to be relative. It seems to me that anyone today who reads this story and concludes that the man deserves punishment for the way he treated his wife must come to terms with how they arrived at such a conclusion.

There are two options. A personal judgment based on emotion, and what might be considered common sense, that inflicting harm on another human being is wrong. To this person I respectfully propose that his emotions and common sense operated according to God's Law as it is written on his heart (Rom. 2:14-15). The other option is the general acknowledgment that man's laws, and what the person who breaks them deserves, is either derived from man or it comes from an ultimate authority. If it's from man, then negligence becomes a defense for the guilty as there is no guarantee that everyone knows what the law is. To this person I propose that they consider that the ultimate authority is God; man's laws are based on God's Law (just as man's words have their origin in God's Word. see John 1:1-3) and He has made it known to all men by writing it on everyone's heart.

The Nail

A merchant had done good business at the fair; he had sold his wares, and lined his money-bags with gold and silver. Then he wanted to travel homewards, and be in his own house before nightfall. So he packed his trunk with the money on his horse, and rode away.

At noon he rested in a town, and when he wanted to go farther the stable-boy brought out his horse and said, "A nail is wanting, sir, in the shoe of its left hind foot."

"Let it be wanting," answered the merchant; "the shoe will certainly stay on for the six miles I have still to go. I am in a hurry."

In the afternoon, when he once more rested and had his horse fed, the stable-boy went into the room to him and said, "Sir, a shoe is missing from your horse's left hind foot. Shall I take him to the blacksmith?"

"Let it still be wanting," answered the man; "the horse can very well hold out for the couple of miles which remain. I am in haste."

He rode forth, but before long the horse began to limp. It had not limped long before it began to stumble, and it had not stumbled long before it fell down and broke its leg. The merchant was forced to leave the horse where it was, and unbuckle the trunk, take it on his back, and go home on foot. And there he did not arrive until quite late at night. "And that unlucky nail," said he to himself, "has caused all this disaster."

Hasten slowly.

* * *

IN this tale the authors state exactly what they wish to teach the reader: "Hasten slowly." *Festina lente*. It's an ancient oxymoronic proverb and apparently one of Augustus' favorite sayings, along with "Better a safe commander than a bold [one]." We find the words of Augustus' strategic military wisdom in God's Word. Proverbs 16:32 says, "Better a patient person than a warrior, one with self-control than one who takes a city."

I was raised with *festina lente* ever in my ears, albeit in a way that relates better with this tale and the practical lesson for the common person than Augustus' quips about commanding an army. While working in the garage or around the house my pop used to tell me that if you take care of your tools, your tools will take care of you.

As a child, I was always in a hurry to get done with chores and didn't realize the value of wiping off the wrench after working on the car. As adult, after years of working in the oilfield, I came to value my instruction on the matter and can testify to the frustration of having to use gummed up or corroded tools. I'm proud to say I learned the lesson (and, as far as shop etiquette goes, I now serve my father according to Prov. 27:11).

The merchant, like some of my co-workers, however, needed more schooling. He didn't take care of his tools, in this case his horse and as my father said, the tool didn't take care of him.

His haste proved to slow him down. Perhaps the modern version of this story is the consideration given to the tires on a person's car. Routine inspection and maintenance keeps the driver on the road and gets him where he needs to be without a problem. Neglect the tires and eventually he'll have to deal with a flat, and usually when he is in a hurry to get somewhere. Just talk to an employee at your local auto parts store and you'll hear the sound wisdom that routine maintenance is the best way to save money and avoid inconvenience, which brings us to the ultimate way the words of this tale find their source in the Word of God. This short story offers instruction on how to live. "Hasten slowly."

Consider James 1:19, "Know this, my beloved brothers: let every person be quick to hear, slow to speak…" How many people are too rushed to listen to that which would greatly benefit them? The stable-boy comes to us and says, "A nail is wanting" and we with our hasty, I-can't-be-bothered-right-now-attitudes, reply, "Let it be wanting… I am in a hurry." Do we hasten slowly? "Your tires are bald," says the mechanic. "You really should get new ones." But after considering the financial pinch a person may well choose to roll the dice, saying, "I can get a couple more miles out of them."

Are you quick to listen and slow to speak, to act? Or is it the other way around. Are you taking care of your tools so that they'll take care of you, wiping off your wrench, making sure it's always ready for use?

The Nail teaches us the same lesson as God's Word. "For the Lord gives wisdom; from his mouth come knowledge and understanding" (Prov. 2:6). It tells us not to be foolish, like our trunk-toting merchant. The stable-boy is like "Christ Jesus, who became to us wisdom from God, righteousness and sanctification and redemption" (1 Cor. 1:30). He tells us (the merchant) the truth of our predicament and He's willing to deal with it on our behalf.

By the grace of God someone says, "Sir, Christ is missing from your life. Shall I take you to the cross–to church?"

And unless we heed his wisdom we say, "Let me be. I can hold out for a while longer. My life's too busy right now. I'm doing pretty good in life–having lined our money-bags with gold and silver– just let me be on my way."

This is the response of a person who's not hastening slowly, who ignores the news that the nail is missing, who doesn't see that the horse is limping –that the tires are bald–the birth pains of things to come (Matt. 24:8). This is the perspective of a fool. What sort of people ought we be, according to the brothers Grimm and according Scripture? People who live in "holiness and godliness, waiting for and hastening the coming of the day of God" (2 Pet. 3:11-12), knowing the wisdom of Scripture before our horse loses a nail, so to speak. We're to be Christians, "not carried away with the error of lawless people [to] lose our stability. But [who] grow in the grace and knowledge of our Lord and Savior Jesus Christ" (2 Pet. 3:17-18). We are to recognize that disaster can be avoided, if only we would hasten slowly, listen, and believe the Word spoken to us.

Tom Thumb

THERE was once a poor peasant who sat in the evening by the hearth and poked the fire, and his wife sat and span. Then he said, "How sad it is that we have no children! With us all is so quiet, and in other houses it is noisy and lively."

"Yes," replied the wife, and sighed, "even if we had only one, and it were quite small, and only as big as a thumb, I should be quite satisfied, and we would still love it with all our hearts."

Now it so happened that the woman fell ill, and after seven months gave birth to a child, that was perfect in all its limbs, but no longer than a thumb. Then they said, "It is as we wished it to be, and it shall be our dear child;" and because of its size, they called it Tom

Thumb. They did not let it want for food, but the child did not grow taller, but remained as it had been at the first, nevertheless it looked sensibly out of its eyes, and soon showed itself to be a wise and nimble creature, for everything it did turned out well.

One day the peasant was getting ready to go into the forest to cut wood, when he said as if to himself, "How I wish that there was someone who would bring the cart to me!"

"Oh father," cried Tom Thumb, "I will soon bring the cart, rely on that; it shall be in the forest at the appointed time."

The man smiled and said, "How can that be done, you are far too small to lead the horse by the reins?"

"That's of no consequence, father, if my mother will only harness it, I shall sit in the horse's ear and call out to him how he is to go."

"Well," answered the man, "for once we will try it."

When the time came, the mother harnessed the horse, and placed Tom Thumb in its ear, and then the little creature cried, "Gee up, gee up!"

Then it went quite properly as if with its master, and the cart went the right way into the forest.

It so happened that just as he was turning a corner, and the little one was crying, "Gee up," two strange men came towards him.

"My word!" said one of them, "What is this? There is a cart coming, and a driver is calling to the horse and still he is not to be seen!"

"That can't be right," said the other, "we will follow the cart and see where it stops."

The cart, however, drove right into the forest, and exactly to the place where the wood had been cut.

When Tom Thumb saw his father, he cried to him, "See, father, here I am with the cart; now take me down."

The father got hold of the horse with his left hand and with the right took his little son out of the ear. Tom Thumb sat down quite merrily on a straw, but when the two strange men saw him, they did not know what to say for astonishment.

Then one of them took the other aside and said, "Listen, the little fellow would make our

Tom Thumb

fortune if we exhibited him in a large town, for money. We will buy him."

They went to the peasant and said, "Sell us the little man. He shall be well treated with us."

"No," replied the father, "he is the apple of my eye, and all the money in the world cannot buy him from me."

Tom Thumb, however, when he heard of the bargain, had crept up the folds of his father's coat, placed himself on his shoulder, and whispered in his ear, "Father do give me away, I will soon come back again."

Then the father parted with him to the two men for a handsome bit of money.

"Where will you sit?" they said to him.

"Oh just set me on the rim of your hat, and then I can walk backwards and forwards and look at the country, and still not fall down."

They did as he wished, and when Tom thumb had taken leave of his father, they went away with him. They walked until it was dusk, and then the little fellow said, "Do take me down, I want to come down."

The man took his hat off, and put the little fellow on the ground by the wayside, and he leapt and crept about a little between the sods, and then he suddenly slipped into a mouse hole which he had sought out.

"Good evening, gentlemen, just go home without me," he cried to them, and mocked them.

They ran there and stuck their sticks into the mouse hole, but it was all lost labor. Tom Thumb crept still farther in, and as it soon became quite dark, they were forced to go home with their vexation and their empty purses.

When Tom Thumb saw that they were gone, he crept back out of the subterranean passage. "It is so dangerous to walk on the ground in the dark," he said; "how easily a neck or a leg is broken!" Fortunately he knocked against an empty snail shell. "Thank God!" he said. "In that I can pass the night in safety," and got into it.

Not long afterwards, when he was just going to sleep, he heard two men go by, and one of them was saying, "How shall we contrive to get hold of the rich pastor's silver and gold?"

"I could tell you that," cried Tom Thumb, interrupting them.

"What was that?" said one of the thieves in fright, "I heard someone speaking."

Tom Thumb

They stood still listening, and Tom Thumb spoke again, and said, "Take me with you, and I'll help you."

"But where are you?"

"Just look on the ground, and observe from where my voice comes," he replied.

There the thieves at length found him, and lifted him up. "You little imp, how will you help us?" they said.

"A great deal," he said, "I will creep into the pastor's room through the iron bars, and will reach out to you whatever you want to have."

"Come then," they said, "and we will see what you can do."

When they got to the pastor's house, Tom Thumb crept into the room, but instantly cried out with all his might, "Do you want to have everything that is here?"

The thieves were alarmed, and said, "But do speak softly, so as not to waken any one!"

Tom Thumb however, behaved as if he had not understood this, and cried again, "What do you want? Do you want to have everything that is here?"

The cook, who slept in the next room, heard this and sat up in bed, and listened. The thieves, however, had in their fright run some distance away, but at last they took courage, and thought, "The little rascal wants to mock us." They came back and whispered to him, "Come, be serious, and reach something out to us."

Then Tom Thumb again cried as loudly as he could, "I really will give you everything, just put your hands in."

The maid who was listening, heard this quite distinctly, and jumped out of bed and rushed to the door. The thieves took flight, and ran as if the Wild Huntsman were behind them, but as the maid could not see anything, she went to strike a light. When she came to the place with it, Tom Thumb, unperceived, betook himself to the granary, and the maid, after she had examined every corner and found nothing, lay down in her bed again, and believed that, after all, she had only been dreaming with open eyes and ears.

Tom Thumb had climbed up among the hay and found a beautiful place to sleep in; there he intended to rest until day, and then go home again to his parents. But he had other things to go through. Truly, there is much affliction and misery in this world!

Tom Thumb

When day dawned, the maid arose from her bed to feed the cows. Her first walk was into the barn, where she laid hold of an armful of hay, and precisely that very one in which poor Tom Thumb was lying asleep. He, however, was sleeping so soundly that he was aware of nothing, and did not awake until he was in the mouth of the cow, who had picked him up with the hay.

"Ah, heavens!" he cried, "how have I got into the fulling mill?" but he soon discovered where he was. Then it was necessary to be careful not to let himself go between the teeth and be dismembered, but he was nevertheless forced to slip down into the stomach with the hay. "In this little room the windows are forgotten," he said, "and no sun shines in, neither will a candle be brought."

His quarters were especially unpleasing to him, and the worst was, more and more hay was always coming in by the door, and the space grew less and less. Then at length in his anguish, he cried as loud as he could, "Bring me no more fodder, bring me no more fodder."

The maid was just milking the cow, and when she heard someone speaking, and saw no one, and perceived that it was the same voice that she had heard in the night, she was so terrified that she slipped off her stool, and spilt the milk. She ran in great haste to her master, and said, "Oh heavens, pastor, the cow has been speaking!"

"You are mad," replied the pastor; but he went himself to the byre to see what was there.

Hardly, however had he set his foot inside when Tom Thumb again cried, "Bring me no more fodder, bring me no more fodder."

Then the pastor himself was alarmed, and thought that an evil spirit had gone into the cow, and ordered her to be killed. She was killed, but the stomach, in which Tom Thumb was, was thrown on the midden. Tom Thumb had great difficulty in working his way; however, he succeeded so far as to get some room, but just as he was going to thrust his head out, a new misfortune occurred. A hungry wolf ran there, and swallowed the whole stomach at one gulp.

Tom Thumb did not lose courage. "Perhaps," he thought, "the wolf will listen to what I have got to say," and he called to him from out of his stomach, "Dear wolf, I know of a magnificent feast for you."

"Where is it to be had?" said the wolf.

Tom Thumb

"In such and such a house; you must creep into it through the kitchen sink, and will find cakes, and bacon, and sausages, and as much of them as you can eat," and he described to him exactly his father's house.

The wolf did not require to be told this twice, squeezed himself in at night through the sink, and ate to his heart's content in the larder. When he had eaten his fill, he wanted to go out again, but he had become so big that he could not go out by the same way. Tom Thumb had reckoned on this, and now began to make a violent noise in the wolf's body, and raged and screamed as loudly as he could.

"Will you be quiet," said the wolf, "you will wake up the people!"

"Eh, what," replied the little fellow, "You have eaten your fill, and I will make merry likewise," and began once more to scream with all his strength.

At last his father and mother were aroused by it, and ran to the room and looked in through the opening in the door. When they saw that a wolf was inside, they ran away, and the husband fetched his axe, and the wife the scythe.

"Stay behind," said the man, when they entered the room. "When I have given him a blow, if he is not killed by it, you must cut him down and hew his body to pieces."

Then Tom Thumb heard his parents voices and cried, "Dear father, I am here; I am in the wolf's body."

Full of joy the father said, "Thank God, our dear child has found us again," and charged the woman to take away her scythe, that Tom Thumb might not be hurt with it.

After that he raised his arm, and struck the wolf such a blow on his head that he fell down dead, and then they got knives and scissors and cut his body open and drew the little fellow forth.

"Ah," said the father, "what sorrow we have gone through for your sake."

"Yes father, I have gone about the world a great deal. Thank heaven, I breathe fresh air again!"

"Where have you been, then?"

"Ah, father, I have been in a mouse's hole, in a cow's stomach, and then in a wolf's; now I will stay with you."

"And we will not sell you again, no, not for all the riches in the world," said his parents, and they embraced and kissed their dear Tom Thumb. They gave him to eat and to drink, and had some new clothes made for him, for his own had been spoiled on his journey.

* * *

TOM Thumb immediately establishes itself as a pro-life story, to use today's terminology. The opening scene is the story of a married couple who cannot conceive and are plagued by the quietness of a home without children, a home that isn't "noisy and lively." The beginning of the tale calls to mind the women of Scripture who struggled with infertility. We certainly hear echoes of the Biblical couples who battled barrenness, such as Sarai and Abram, Rebekah and Isaac, and Rachel and Jacob.

One Biblical account echoes louder in my mind than the others. Hannah and Elkanah, the couple that would eventually conceive Samuel. Tom Thumb's mother was sad to have no children as was Hannah. You can almost hear Hannah's lament in the her voice, "With us all is so quiet, and in other houses it is noisy and lively." Hannah was provoked by her husband's other wife who had children. The peasant's wife lived in a similar state of comparative torment.

Like Hannah, vowing what she would do should the Lord give her a son (1 Sam. 1:11), the peasant's wife says with a sigh, "even if we had only one, and it were quite small, and only as big as a thumb, I should be quite satisfied, and we would still love it with all our hearts."

It doesn't matter to her if the child isn't like other children, she would love it just the same. Let the baby be what it will be, she will be mother. In a day and age where prenatal testing is often abused so that a mother can murder her child if an abnormality is discovered a tale of a mother's love no matter what the circumstance is a breath of fresh air.

This is a story of life emerging from the place of death. Like Hannah, the peasant's barren wife eventually gives birth to a son, though he is as small as a thumb. Big things come in small packages. God, the life of the world came into the world (John 1:1-10) in the form of an infant born of Mary, the Son sent from the Father to save the world (John 3:16-17).

Jesus was the Father's only Son and yet He was given to do what only He could do. And what He did, dying on the cross to forgive sins, He did willingly (John 10:18). In the same way, Tom was willing to go into the world. "Father," Tom Thumb said, "do give me away, I will soon come back again."

Christ's willingness to go to the grave is found all throughout His earthly life. He faced insult and injury at every turn, yet He pushed forward, continuously focused on His task of removing the hurt from the world, of establishing the means by which death would be swallowed up forever (Is. 25:8). He set His face toward Jerusalem, toward the cross (Luke 9:51). In the words of Tom's adventure, "he had other things to go through. Truly, there is much affliction and misery in the world!"

The entire story of this little thumbling is the story of Jesus going into the tomb as an act of sacrificial service. This point begins to surface when Tom goes with the two strangers. At dusk (Mark 15:42) he says, "Do take me down, I want to come down." Is it merely down from riding atop a hat, or is it down from heaven to save the world, which is ultimately down from the cross to be buried in the tomb for three days before being resurrected?

Tom is let down and slips into a mouse hole. He goes deep into the darkness of the hole. Christ went deep into the darkness of the grave as well. As we confess in the Apostles' Creed, He descended into hell (1 Pet. 3:19-20). Like Jesus, Tom doesn't stay entombed in the earth, but "crept back out of the subterranean passage."

From here we're immersed in the sign of Jonah, "For just as Jonah was three days and three nights in the belly of the great fish, so will the Son of Man be three days and three nights in the heart of the earth" (Matt. 12:40). And just as Jesus was indeed three days and three nights in the heart of the earth Tom Thumb was in the belly of a cow and a wolf.

If you will permit me, for but a moment, to consider what the Father might have asked Jesus when He ascended into heaven, there is a splendidly comforting connection to be made between this story and the truth of Scripture. To do so we will have to pretend God doesn't have all His divine attributes. But if it is permissible we will uncover a way in which the imaginative words of the brothers Grimm attempt to paint a picture of Jesus and heaven and life immortal. Imagine the conversation

Tom has with his dad to be that of Jesus and His Father.

"Ah," said the Father, "what sorrow we have gone through for your sake."

"Yes Father, I have gone about the world a great deal. Thank heaven, I breathe fresh air again!"

"Where have you been, then?"

"Ah, Father, I have been in a mouse's hole, in a cow's stomach, and then in a wolf's [that is to say, I was killed, laid in a tomb, and descended into hell]; now I will stay with you."

The Christian reader knows that our Father in heaven wasn't ignorant of what Jesus went through while living on earth. However, allowing the imagination to work with such a notion enables us to read the reunion conversation in the story of Tom Thumb the way we read Jesus' parable of the prodigal son, which has similar elements, namely new clothing and eating in celebration (Luke 15:22-24) because the son who was dead is alive again. The father in Jesus' parable *embraced* his son and *kissed* him. These words are used by the Grimm brothers of Tom's parents before they "gave him to eat and to drink, and had some new clothes made for him, for his own had been spoiled on his journey." Exactly what happened to the lost son in Jesus' parable.

This tale delivers the Biblical truth of heaven, which we, even now, experience when we celebrate Communion, the foretaste of the feast to come, as Revelation says, when "the marriage of the Lamb has come, and his Bride has made herself ready; it was granted her to clothe herself with fine linen, bright and pure'– for the fine linen is the righteous deeds of the saints." and "blessed are those who are invited to the marriage supper of the Lamb" (Rev. 19:7-9).

I love how this story ends. I love that Tom eats and drinks–feasts–and I love how he gets "new clothes made for him, for his own had been spoiled on his journey." This is what the Christian looks forward to as a believer who, in baptism, has put on the new clothes of Christ (Gal. 3:27; Rom. 13:14). Apart from Jesus, what I'm wearing has been spoiled on my journey through life. I'm a sinner living in a sinful world. I need new threads. In Baptism into Christ, into His death and resurrection, into His righteousness, I have them. I have a garment that allows me to sit at the table where I can eat (Matt. 22:2,11-14). The picture of what Tom experiences in the last sentence of his story is a picture of what we've been told will happen to the Christian in 1 Corinthians 15:50-58, when the perishable body will put on the imperishable and the mortal body the immortal, or in other words, the spoiled will, in Christ, put on the un-spoilable.

> I tell you this, brothers: flesh and blood cannot inherit the kingdom of God, nor does the perishable inherit the imperishable. Behold! I tell you a mystery. We shall not all sleep, but we shall all be changed, in a moment, in the twinkling of an eye, at the last trumpet. For the trumpet will sound, and the dead will be raised imperishable, and we shall be changed. For this perishable body must put on the imperishable, and this mortal body must put on immortality. When the perishable puts on the imperishable, and the mortal puts on immortality, then shall come to pass the saying that is written: 'Death is swallowed up in victory.' 'O death, where is your victory? O death, where is your sting?'" (1 Cor. 15:50-58).

Tom Thumb, Journeyman

A certain tailor had a son, who happened to be small, and no bigger than a Thumb, and on this account he was always called Tom Thumb. He had, however, some courage in him, and said to his father, "Father, I must and will go out into the world."

"That's right, my son," said the old man, and took a long darning needle and made a knob of sealing wax on it at the candle, "and there is a sword for you to take with you on the way."

Then the little tailor wanted to have one more meal with them, and hopped into the kitchen to see what his lady mother had cooked for the last time. It was, however, just dished

Tom Thumb, Journeyman

up, and the dish stood on the hearth. Then he said, "Mother, what is there to eat today?"

"See for yourself," said his mother.

So Tom Thumb jumped on to the hearth, and peeped into the dish, but as he stretched his neck in too far the steam from the food caught hold of him, and carried him up the chimney. He rode about in the air on the steam for a while, until at length he sank down to the ground again. Now the little tailor was outside in the wide world, and he travelled about, and went to a master in his craft, but the food was not good enough for him.

"Mistress, if you give us no better food," said Tom Thumb, "I will go away, and early tomorrow morning I will write with chalk on the door of your house, 'Too many potatoes, too little meat! Farewell, Mr. Potato King.'"

"What would you have in truth, grasshopper?" said the mistress, and grew angry, and seized a dishcloth, and was just going to strike him; but my little tailor crept nimbly under a thimble, peeped out from beneath it, and put his tongue out at the mistress. She took up the thimble, and wanted to get hold of him, but little Tom Thumb hopped into the cloth, and while the mistress was opening it out and looking for him, he got into a crevice in the table.

"Ho, ho, lady mistress," he cried, and thrust his head out, and when she began to strike him he leapt down into the drawer.

At last, however, she caught him and drove him out of the house.

The little tailor journeyed on and came to a great forest, and there he fell in with a band of robbers who had a design to steal the King's treasure. When they saw the little tailor, they thought, "A little fellow like that can creep through a keyhole and serve as picklock to us."

"Hollo," cried one of them, "you giant Goliath, will you go to the treasure chamber with us? You can slip yourself in and throw out the money."

Tom Thumb reflected a while, and at length he said, "yes," and went with them to the treasure chamber.

Then he looked at the doors above and below, to see if there was any crack in them. It was not long before he spied one which was broad enough to let him in. He was therefore about to get in at once, but one of the two sentries who stood before the door, observed

Tom Thumb, Journeyman

him, and said to the other, "What an ugly spider is creeping there; I will kill it."

"Let the poor creature alone," said the other; "it has done you no harm."

Then Tom Thumb got safely through the crevice into the treasure chamber, opened the window beneath which the robbers were standing, and threw out to them one thaler after another. When the little tailor was in the full swing of his work, he heard the King coming to inspect his treasure chamber, and crept hastily into a hiding place.

The King noticed that several solid thalers were missing, but could not conceive who could have stolen them, for locks and bolts were in good condition, and all seemed well guarded. Then he went away again, and said to the sentries, "Be on the watch, someone is after the money."

When therefore Tom Thumb recommenced his labors, they heard the money moving, and a sound of klink, klink, klink. They ran swiftly in to seize the thief, but the little tailor, who heard them coming, was still swifter, and leapt into a corner and covered himself with a thaler, so that nothing could be seen of him, and at the same time he mocked the sentries and cried,

"Here am I!" The sentries ran there, but as they got there, he had already hopped into another corner under a thaler, and was crying, "Ho, ho, here am I!" The watchmen sprang there in haste, but Tom Thumb had long ago got into a third corner, and was crying, "Ho, ho, here am I!" And thus he made fools of them, and drove them so long round about the treasure chamber that they were weary and went away. Then by degrees he threw all the thalers out, dispatching the last with all his might, then hopped nimbly upon it, and flew down with it through the window.

The robbers paid him great compliments. "You are valiant hero," they said; "will you be our captain?"

Tom Thumb, however, declined, and said he wanted to see the world first. They now divided the booty, but the little tailor only asked for a kreuzer because he could not carry more.

Then he once more buckled on his sword, bade the robbers goodbye, and took to the road. First, he went to work with some masters, but he had no liking for that, and at last he hired himself as manservant in an inn. The maids, however, could not endure him, for he saw all

Tom Thumb, Journeyman

they did secretly, without their seeing him, and he told their master and mistress what they had taken off the plates, and carried away out of the cellar, for themselves.

Then they said, "Wait, and we will pay you off!" and arranged with each other to play him a trick. Soon afterwards when one of the maids was mowing in the garden, and saw Tom Thumb jumping about and creeping up and down the plants, she mowed him up quickly with the grass, tied all in a great cloth, and secretly threw it to the cows. Now among them there was a great black one, who swallowed him down without hurting him. Down below, however, it pleased him ill, for it was quite dark, neither was any candle burning. When the cow was being milked he cried,

*"Strip, strap, strull,
Will the pail soon be full?"*

But the noise of the milking prevented his being understood. After this the master of the house came into the cow byre and said, "That cow shall be killed tomorrow."

Then Tom Thumb was so alarmed that he cried out in a clear voice, "Let me out first, for I am shut up inside her."

The master heard that quite well, but did not know from where the voice came. "Where are you?" he asked.

"In the black one," answered Tom Thumb, but the master did not understand what that meant, and went out.

Next morning the cow was killed. Happily Tom Thumb did not meet with one blow at the cutting up and chopping; he got among the sausage meat. And when the butcher came in and began his work, he cried out with all his might, "Don't chop too deep, don't chop too deep, I am among it." No one heard this because of the noise of the chopping knife.

Now poor Tom Thumb was in trouble, but trouble sharpens the wits, and he sprang out so skillfully between the blows that none of them touched him, and he escaped with a whole skin. But still he could not get away, there was nothing for it but to let himself be thrust into a black pudding with the bits of bacon. His quarters there were rather confined, and besides that he was hung up in the chimney to be smoked, and there time did hang terribly heavy on his hands.

At length in winter he was taken down again, as the black pudding had to be set before a guest. When the hostess was cutting it in slices, he took care not to stretch out his head too far lest a bit of it should be cut off; at last he saw his opportunity, cleared a passage for himself, and jumped out.

The little tailor, however, would not stay any longer in a house where he fared so ill, so at once set out on his journey again. But his liberty did not last long. In the open country he met with a fox who snapped him up in a fit of absence.

"Hollo, Mr. Fox," cried the little tailor, "it is I who am sticking in your throat, set me at liberty again."

"You are right," answered the fox. "You are next to nothing for me, but if you will promise me the fowls in your father's yard I will let you go."

"With all my heart," replied Tom Thumb. "You shall have all the cocks and hens, that I promise you."

Then the fox let him go again, and himself carried him home. When the father once more saw his dear son, he willingly gave the fox all the fowls which he had.

"For this I likewise bring you a handsome bit of money," said Tom Thumb, and gave his father the kreuzer which he earned on his travels.

"But why did the fox get the poor chickens to eat?"

"Oh, you goose, your father would surely love his child far more than the fowls in the yard!"

* * *

TOM Thumb is a fascinating person. Should time allow, someday I would like to study his history. Other than what the Grimm Brothers have preserved for us, is there anything more to know about the creation of this amazing protagonist? For now, however, Tom's Grimm adventures will suffice. There is plenty to keep us engaged.

It's interesting to note that the *Journeyman* story follows a similar plot line as the previous Tom Thumb tale. He leaves his parents, gets entangled in the happenings of some robbers, is swallowed by a cow, and even finds his way into a canine's mouth before making his way back to his father.

The Christological motif of death and resurrection is certainly present in this story. At first I thought that perhaps *Journeyman* was nothing more than a retelling, a reboot if you will, of the same story, but upon further consideration I abandoned that notion and came to think of it as a sequel. In the *Tom Thumb* chapter I referred to similarities between the Bible's Hannah and the peasant's wife, specifically their desire to be mothers. That's just the beginning. Tom Thumb would appear to be Samuel's fairyland counterpart.

Eventually both women conceived children, Samuel and Tom. Hannah did as she had vowed and gave Samuel back to the Lord (1 Sam. 1:11, 27-28). Likewise, Tom's mother did as she said she would and loved him with all her heart. Samuel left Hannah's care when she brought him to the house of the Lord with the food stuffs for an offering (1 Sam. 1:24) where the priests would've eaten a portion of part of it (Lev. 2:3). Tom left his mother's care when upon the hearth he looked into the dish she had prepared and was carried up the chimney by "the steam from the food," the steam that would have carried the scent of the meal, or in offering language the "pleasing aroma to the Lord" (Num. 15:10).

This aromatic steam carried Tom up into the air, drawing the Biblically literate reader to the offering that accompanied Samuel on his journey. When Tom "sank down to the ground again" he "went to a master in his craft, but the food was not good enough for him." It may be hard to see the parallel at first, but this is nothing other than Samuel being delivered to Eli.

In Samuel's story, after we're told that "the boy ministered to the Lord in the presence of Eli the priest" (1 Sam. 2:11) we hear about the poor behavior of Eli's sons (1 Sam. 2:12-17). They were taking the priestly share of the offerings "before the fat was burned" (1 Sam. 2:15), in other words, before the Lord had been given His portion (Lev. 3:3–5; 7:30). Eating the fat from the sacrificial animals was an act explicitly prohibited (Lev. 7:22–26) and to top it off, they used the threat of violence to get their way. In the words of the brothers Grimm, "the food [read offering] was not good enough." It had "too many potatoes, too little meat!" A poor offering indeed. Eli's sons abused their position and didn't serve the Israelites and the Lord as they should have.

When Tom confronted the mistress about the atrocity, what did she use but the threat of violence to drive him away. Avoiding her angry strikes lead him to journey to a great forest where "he fell in with a band of robbers." This is the second time he worked with thieves. In the first tale he protected a pastor's silver and gold while in the company of robbers, but in this story he actually assists the robbers in stealing the King's money. Curious.

As masters in their craft, the Grimms creatively conflated two Biblical texts delivering a great story rooted in the Word: the Lord calling Samuel (1 Sam. 3) and Samuel issuing a warning against having kings (1 Sam. 8:10-18). Why would Tom steal from the King? A clue to his motivation is given when the robbers greet him, "you giant Goliath, will you go to the treasure chamber with us?"

Goliath?

Rest assured this is more than just the use of an ironic nickname, although it is certainly that as well. Goliath was a Philistine, and though he's not immediately involved in Samuel's story, he was the quintessential representation of his people. This little greeting provides context. Packed into the word *Goliath* is the conflict between the Philistines and the Hebrews that is conveyed between chapters three and eight of 1 Samuel. The Grimms combined those two chapters. It's the Philistines who attack Israel, at which time Eli's sons, the meat stealing Potato-Kings, die (1 Sam. 4:10-11).

Tom's working against an earthly king extends from Samuel warning the people about having earthly kings after Israel had rejected the Lord as their king (1 Sam. 8:7). In our fairy tale the King is a bad guy, a usurper who has taken the place of the real King, God. What does Samuel do but speak against the establishment of a king, against the king taking for himself that which is Israel's and storing up the kingdom's treasures for himself? Tom is merely taking back what the earthly king took from God's people – from God. This is clearly seen in what Tom does with the "kreuzer, which he earned on his travels." He gives it to his father. The treasure that was taken from God when Israel rejected Him is given back to Him when His Son returns home – Tom, in this case, is both a Samuel figure and a Christ figure, just as the prophet's mouth speaks the Word of the Lord.

In Scripture the warning comes after Samuel is called to be a prophet of the Lord (1 Sam. 3). This happened in a very memorable way when the Lord called Samuel, and three times he answered by saying, "Here am I" (1 Sam. 3:4-5, 6-7, 8-9). Finally, Eli perceives that it's the Lord calling Samuel.

In the words of the Grimms, however, this threefold, "Here am I," occurs, not before, but as part of the robbery of the earthly King. Nevertheless, the point is made that the words of this tale extend from the Word of God recorded in 1 Samuel.

If you aren't familiar with it, perhaps now would be a good time to take a peak. As much as I like Tom's adventures, Samuel's are much better, plus they're true.

Sweet Porridge

THERE was a poor but good little girl who lived alone with her mother, and they no longer had anything to eat. So the child went into the forest, and there an aged woman met her who was aware of her sorrow, and presented her with a little pot, which when she said, "Cook, little pot, cook," would cook good, sweet porridge, and when she said, "Stop, little pot," it ceased to cook.

The girl took the pot home to her mother, and they were freed from their poverty and hunger, and ate sweet porridge as often as they chose.

Once on a time when the girl had gone out, her mother said, "Cook, little pot, cook." And it did cook and she ate till she was satisfied, and then she wanted the pot to stop cooking, but did not know the word. So it went on cooking and the porridge rose over the edge, and still it cooked on until the kitchen and whole house were full, and then the next house, and then the whole street, just as if it wanted to satisfy the hunger of the whole world, and there was the greatest distress, but no one knew how to stop it.

At last when only one single house remained, the child came home and just said, "Stop, little pot," and it stopped and gave up cooking, and whosoever wished to return to the town had to eat his way back.

* * *

AH, sweet porridge. It can be said that all the problems and remedies of life find their root in food. Do you have it or not? To have food for the day is to be content (1 Tim. 6:8). When it comes to earthly provisions, what more are we to desire? Like Agur, son of Jakeh, the Christian says to God, "give me neither poverty nor riches; feed me with the food that is needful for me, lest I be full and deny you and say, 'Who is the Lord?' or lest I be poor and steal and profane the name of my God." (Prov.30:8-9)

Every time we pray the Lord's Prayer this is what we're saying: "give us this day our daily bread." (Matt.6:11) "Cook little pot, cook." That's what this story is about, right? The cooking of a little pot. The giving of daily bread – sweet porridge. It's about our daily needs being provided for, as the "poor but good little girl who lived alone with her mother... no longer had anything to eat" and yet she was given daily bread in the form of sweet porridge, and she was given it miraculously and often – her daily bread turned out to be a gift given abundantly.

This calls to mind the words of 2 Corinthians 9:8-10,

> And God is able to make grace abound to you, so that having all sufficiency in all things at all times, you may abound in every good work. As it is written, 'He has *distributed freely*, he has *given to the poor*; his righteousness endures forever.' He who supplies seed to the sower and bread for food will supply and *multiply* your seed for

Sweet Porridge

> sowing and increase the harvest of your righteousness." (Emphasis mine)

You see, "the poor but *good* [read faith-filled] little girl" received her daily bread, which was distributed to her freely and multiplied, becoming a blessing for more than just her and her mother.

> ...her mother said, 'Cook, little pot, cook." And it did cook and she ate till she was satisfied, and then she wanted the pot to stop cooking, but did not know the word. So it went on cooking and the porridge rose over the edge, and still it cooked on until the kitchen and whole house were full, and then the next house, and then the whole street, just as if it wanted to satisfy the hunger of the whole world...

What a remarkable story! A food that spreads "as if it wanted to satisfy the hunger of the whole world." A food that spreads according to a familiar pattern: house, the next house, and then the whole street.

What was it that Jesus said to the disciples at the beginning of Acts? Oh yes, "But you will receive power when the Holy Spirit has come upon you, and you will be my witnesses in Jerusalem (house), and in all Judea and Samaria (next house), and to the end of the earth (whole street)." (Acts 1:8) This sweet porridge spreads as if it wants to satisfy the hunger of the whole world.

May I suggest that we see this as the Word of God spreading across the whole world by the power of the Holy Spirit (despite our sin – witting and unwitting attempts to stop it) in order to satisfy the spiritual hunger of a world in the midst of a great famine, a world in desperate need of receiving God's grace through the means by which He gives it: His Word, Baptism, and the Lord's Supper?

All the problems and remedies of life find their root in whether or not one has food – the nourishment necessary to grow and live. This is a reoccurring theme in Scripture, a theme that leaps off the pages of holy writ and into the mouth of the person kneeling at the altar rail. Keep in mind that man does not live by bread alone, but by every word that comes from the mouth of God (Deut. 8:3; Matt. 4:4).

As the sweet porridge of God's Word spreads throughout the world it is

Sweet Porridge

consumed by hungry hearts (Jer. 3:15; Eze. 3:1-3) and swallowing mouths in the Lord's Supper. Jesus told the disciples that the Holy Spirit would come upon them and they would be His witnesses in the house (Jerusalem), and in the next house (Judea and Samaria), and then the whole street (the end of the earth) as the porridge (Gospel) spread. We see what that looks like after the Holy Spirit comes. "And they devoted themselves to the apostles' teaching and the fellowship, to the *breaking of bread* [or shall we say the scooping of porridge?] and the prayers (Acts 2:42).

The world has become a place covered by Christ, the Word of God, the sweet porridge that freed the poor little girl and her mother from their poverty and hunger, the Gospel truth that sets us free from sin, saves us from death, and gives us eternal life. In the days of the Grimm brothers and, yes, even today, despite our attempts to stop it, Christianity abounds. It has truly covered the whole world in sweet porridge. It's in the nooks and crannies of how people think and believe. A person does not have to believe in Christ to live in this world, but should he try to return the world to a pre-Christian state, he couldn't just stroll back to town, to a worldview void of God's Word. No, like the Grimm tale tells us, "whoever wished to return to the town had to eat his way back."

The little pot has cooked and the only thing a person can do is eat. We can eat as often as we choose, till we are satisfied (Matt. 14:20), receiving the blessings of such a sweet porridge, or we can eat in an effort to rid the world of true food, to bring about a famine. But to do so one must dine on the truth of Christ. Either way, Jesus will be consumed. He has come into the world. There is no undoing that. The little pot has cooked.[21]

---

[21] This was a broad approach to Sweet Porridge. For a narrow handling of the story the interested reader may wish to study the parallels between this tale and the historical happening that occurred between Elijah and the widow of Zarephath in 1 Kings 17:8-16.

The Young Giant

ONCE on a time a countryman had a son who was as big as a thumb, and did not become any bigger, and during several years did not grow one hair's breadth. Once when the father was going out to plough, the little one said, "Father, I will go out with you."

"You would go out with me?" said the father. "Stay here, you will be of no use out there, besides you might get lost!"

Then Tom Thumb began to cry, and for the sake of peace his father put him in his pocket, and took him with him.

When he was outside in the field, he took him out again, and set him in a freshly cut furrow. While he was there, a great giant came over the hill. "Do you see that great bogie?"

said the father, for he wanted to frighten the little fellow to make him good; "he is coming to fetch you."

The giant, however, had scarcely taken two steps with his long legs before he was in the furrow. He took up little Tom Thumb carefully with two fingers, examined him, and without saying one word went away with him. His father stood by, but could not utter a sound for terror, and he thought nothing else but that his child was lost, and that as long as he lived he should never set eyes on him again.

The giant, however, carried him home, suckled him, and Tom Thumb grew and became tall and strong after the manner of giants. When two years had passed, the old giant took him into the forest, wanted to try him, and said, "Pull up a stick for yourself." Then the boy was already so strong that he tore up a young tree out of the earth by the roots. But the giant thought, "We must do better than that," took him back again, and suckled him two years longer.

When he tried him, his strength had increased so much that he could tear an old tree out of the ground. That was still not enough for the giant; he again suckled him for two years,

The Young Giant

and when he then went with him into the forest and said, "Now just tear up a proper stick for me," the boy tore up the strongest oak tree from the earth, so that it split, and that was a mere trifle to him. "Now that will do," said the giant, "you are perfect," and took him back to the field from where he had brought him.

His father was there following the plough.

The young giant went up to him, and said, "Does my father see what a fine man his son has grown into?"

The farmer was alarmed, and said, "No, you are not my son; I don't want you – leave me!"

"Truly I am your son; allow me to do your work, I can plough as well as you, no, better."

"No, no, you are not my son; and you cannot plough – go away!" However, as he was afraid of this great man, he let go of the plough, stepped back and stood at one side of the piece of land.

Then the youth took the plough, and just pressed it with one hand, but his grasp was so strong that the plough went deep into the earth.

The farmer could not bear to see that, and called to him, "If you are determined to plough, you must not press so hard on it, that makes bad work."

The youth, however, unharnessed the horses, and drew the plough himself, saying, "Just go home, father, and bid my mother make ready a large dish of food, and in the meantime I will go over the field."

Then the farmer went home, and ordered his wife to prepare the food; but the youth ploughed the field which was two acres large, quite alone, and then he harnessed himself to the harrow, and harrowed the whole of the land, using two harrows at once. When he had done it, he went into the forest, and pulled up two oak trees, laid them across his shoulders, and hung on them one harrow behind and one before, and also one horse behind and one before, and carried all as if it had been a bundle of straw, to his parents' house.

When he entered the yard, his mother did not recognize him, and asked, "Who is that horrible tall man?"

The farmer said, "That is our son."

She said, "No that cannot be our son, we never had such a tall one, ours was a little thing." She called to him, "Go away, we do not want you!"

The youth was silent, but led his horses to the stable, gave them some oats and hay, and

The Young Giant

all that they wanted. When he had done this, he went into the parlor, sat down on the bench and said, "Mother, now I should like something to eat, will it soon be ready?"

Then she said, "Yes," and brought in two immense dishes full of food, which would have been enough to satisfy herself and her husband for a week. The youth, however, ate the whole of it himself, and asked if she had nothing more to set before him. "No," she replied, "that is all we have."

"But that was only a taste, I must have more."

She did not dare to oppose him, and went and put a huge caldron full of food on the fire, and when it was ready, carried it in.

"At length come a few crumbs," he said, and ate all there was, but it was still not sufficient to appease his hunger. Then he said, "Father, I see well that with you I shall never have food enough; if you will get me an iron staff which is strong, and which I cannot break against my knees, I will go out into the world."

The farmer was glad, put his two horses in his cart, and fetched from the smith a staff so large and thick, that the two horses could only just bring it away. The youth laid it across his knees, and snap! he broke it in two in the middle like a beanstalk, and threw it away.

The father then harnessed four horses, and brought a bar which was so long and thick, that the four horses could only just drag it. The son snapped this also in two against his knees, threw it away, and said, "Father, this can be of no use to me, you must harness more horses, and bring a stronger staff."

So the father harnessed eight horses, and brought one which was so long and thick, that the eight horses could only just carry it. When the son took it in his hand, he broke off a bit from the top of it also, and said, "Father, I see that you will not be able to procure me any such staff as I want, I will remain no longer with you."

So he went away, and gave out that he was a smith's apprentice. He arrived at a village, wherein lived a smith who was a greedy fellow, who never did a kindness to anyone, but wanted everything for himself. The youth went into the smithy and asked if he needed a journeyman.

"Yes," said the smith, and looked at him, and thought, "That is a strong fellow who will

The Young Giant

strike out well, and earn his bread." So he asked, "How much wages do you want?"

"I don't want any at all," he replied, "only every two weeks, when the other journeymen are paid, I will give you two blows, and you must bear them."

The miser was heartily satisfied, and thought he would therefore save much money.

The next morning, the strange journeyman was to begin to work, but when the master brought the glowing bar, and the youth struck his first blow, the iron flew asunder, and the anvil sank so deep into the earth, that there was no bringing it out again. Then the miser grew angry, and said, "Oh, but I can't make any use of you, you strike far too powerfully; what will you have for the one blow?"

Then he said, "I will only give you quite a small blow, that's all." And he raised his foot, and gave him such a kick that he flew away over four loads of hay. Then he sought out the thickest iron bar in the smithy for himself, took it as a stick in his hand and went onwards.

When he had walked for some time, he came to a small farm, and asked the bailiff if he did not require a head servant.

"Yes," said the bailiff, "I can make use of one; you look a strong fellow who can do something, how much a year do you want as wages?"

He again replied that he wanted no wages at all, but that every year he would give him three blows, which he must bear. Then the bailiff was satisfied, for he, too, was a covetous fellow.

The next morning all the servants were to go into the wood, and the others were already up, but the head servant was still in bed. Then one of them called to him, "Get up, it is time; we are going into the wood, and you must go with us."

"Ah," he said quite roughly and surlily, "you may just go, then; I shall be back again before any of you."

Then the others went to the bailiff, and told him that the head man was still lying in bed, and would not go into the wood with them. The bailiff said they were to awaken him again, and tell him to harness the horses. The head man, however, said as before, "Just go there, I shall be back again before any of you." And then he stayed in bed two hours longer.

The Young Giant

At length he arose from the feathers, but first he got himself two bushels of peas from the loft, made himself some broth with them, ate it at his leisure, and when that was done, went and harnessed the horses, and drove into the wood.

Not far from the wood was a ravine through which he had to pass, so he first drove the horses on, and then stopped them, and went behind the cart, took trees and brushwood, and made a great barricade, so that no horse could get through. When he was entering the wood, the others were just driving out of it with their loaded carts to go home; then said he to them, "Drive on, I will still get home before you do." He did not drive far into the wood, but at once tore two of the very largest trees of all out of the earth, threw them on his cart, and turned around.

When he came to the barricade, the others were still standing there, not able to get through. "Don't you see," he said, "that if you had stayed with me, you would have got home just as quickly, and would have had another hour's sleep?"

He now wanted to drive on, but his horses could not work their way through, so he unharnessed them, laid them on the top of the cart, took the shafts in his own hands, and pulled it all through, and he did this just as easily as if it had been laden with feathers. When he was over, he said to the others, "There, you see, I have got over quicker than you," and drove on, and the others had to stay where they were. In the yard, however, he took a tree in his hand, showed it to the bailiff, and said, "Isn't that a fine bundle of wood?"

Then the bailiff said to his wife, "The servant is a good one, if he does sleep long, he is still home before the others."

So he served the bailiff for a year, and when that was over, and the other servants were getting their wages, he said it was time for him to take his too. The bailiff, however, was afraid of the blows which he was to receive, and earnestly entreated him to excuse him from having them; for rather than that, he himself would be head servant, and the youth should be bailiff.

"No," he said, "I will not be a bailiff, I am head servant, and will remain so, but I will administer that which we agreed on."

The bailiff was willing to give him whatsoever he demanded, but it was of no use,

The Young Giant

the head servant said no to everything. Then the bailiff did not know what to do, and begged for a two week's delay, for he wanted to find some way of escape. The head servant consented to this delay. The bailiff summoned all his clerks together, and they were to think the matter over, and give him advice. The clerks pondered for a long time, but at last they said that no one was sure of his life with the head servant, for he could kill a man as easily as a midge, and that the bailiff ought to make him get into the well and clean it, and when he was down below, they would roll up one of the millstones which was lying there, and throw it on his head; and then he would never return to daylight.

The advice pleased the bailiff, and the head servant was quite willing to go down the well. When he was standing down below at the bottom, they rolled down the largest millstone and thought they had broken his skull, but he cried, "Chase away those hens from the well, they are scratching in the sand up there, and throwing the grains into my eyes, so that I can't see."

So the bailiff cried, "Sh-sh," and pretended to frighten the hens away.

When the head servant had finished his work, he climbed up and said, "Just look what a beautiful neck tie I have on," and behold it was the millstone which he was wearing around his neck. The head servant now wanted to take his reward, but the bailiff again begged for a two week's delay.

The clerks met together and advised him to send the head servant to the haunted mill to grind corn by night, for from there as yet no man had ever returned in the morning alive. The proposal pleased the bailiff, he called the head servant that very evening, and ordered him to take eight bushels of corn to the mill, and grind it that night, for it was wanted.

So the head servant went to the loft, and put two bushels in his right pocket, and two in his left, and took four in a wallet, half on his back, and half on his breast, and thus laden went to the haunted mill. The miller told him that he could grind there very well by day, but not by night, for the mill was haunted, and that up to the present time whosoever had gone into it at night had been found in the morning lying dead inside. He said, "I will manage it, just you go away to bed." Then he went into the mill, and poured out the corn.

The Young Giant

At about eleven o'clock he went into the miller's room, and sat down on the bench. When he had sat there a while, a door suddenly opened, and a large table came in, and on the table, wine and roasted meats placed themselves, and much good food besides, but everything came of itself, for no one was there to carry it. After this the chairs pushed themselves up, but no people came, until all at once he beheld fingers, which handled knives and forks, and laid food on the plates, but with this exception he saw nothing. As he was hungry, and saw the food, he, too, place himself at the table, ate with those who were eating and enjoyed it.

When he had had enough, and the others also had quite emptied their dishes, he distinctly heard all the candles being suddenly snuffed out, and as it was now pitch dark, he felt something like a box on the ear. Then he said, "If anything of that kind comes again, I shall strike out in return." And when he had received a second box on the ear, he, too struck out. And so it continued the whole night. He took nothing without returning it, but repaid everything with interest, and did not lay about him in vain.

At daybreak, however, everything ceased. When the miller had got up, he wanted to look after him, and wondered if he were still alive. Then the youth said, "I have eaten my fill, have received some boxes on the ears, but I have given some in return."

The miller rejoiced, and said that the mill was now released from the spell, and wanted to give him much money as a reward.

But he said, "Money, I will not have, I have enough of it." So he took his meal on his back, went home, and told the bailiff that he had done what he had been told to do, and would now have the reward agreed on.

When the bailiff heard that, he was seriously alarmed and quite beside himself; he walked backwards and forwards in the room, and drops of perspiration ran down from his forehead. Then he opened the window to get some fresh air, but before he was aware, the head servant had given him such a kick that he flew through the window out into the air, and so far away that no one ever saw him again. Then said the head servant to the bailiff's wife, "If he does not come back, you must take the other blow."

The Young Giant

She cried, "No, no I cannot bear it," and opened the other window, because drops of perspiration were running down her forehead.

Then he gave her such a kick that she, too, flew out, and as she was lighter she went much higher than her husband.

Her husband cried, "Do come to me," but she replied, "You come to me, I cannot come to you."

And they hovered about there in the air, and could not get to each other, and whether they are still hovering about, or not, I do not know, but the young giant took up his iron bar, and went on his way.

* * *

THIS is a delightfully bizarre tale featuring Tom Thumb. Only this time the thumbling has been nourished by a giant and is large and strong. It's quite enjoyable, yes, enjoyable to think about his strange desire to deliver blows to those he interacts with, for this story is a creative expression of the theology of the cross.

God chose to save mankind through weakness and shame, through Jesus' detestable and cursed death on a cross (Gal. 3:13). Is this what the Grimm brothers were getting at when they wrote of Tom being sent from the giant into the forest to "tear up a proper stick"? We've already seen how the forest stands in for the world (see *The Frog-King* chapter) and how a giant is a fitting representation of God (see *The Giant and the Tailor* chapter). Likewise, it's not hard to come to the conclusion that the strongest oak tree, which the boy, in a trifle act, tears up from the earth and splits, is a type of crucifixion. Just consider the giant's reaction to such a feat: "Now that will do," said the giant, "you are *perfect*." (emphasis mine)

Nothing else will do to save sinful man from his sins, but the *perfect* death of Jesus on a tree.

Without knowing more about the Grimm brothers, I can't speak with any certainty on the matter, however, I wonder if the 8th century story of Saint Boniface chopping down Thor's Oak, the sacred tree of the Germanic pagans, stirred in the back of the minds of these German brothers (or whomever originally conceived this tale) when it was penned. It was a mere trifle for Jesus to fell the pagan worship of Thor. Indeed!

Christ bore a cross and His followers do too: "Jesus told his disciples, 'If anyone would come after me, let him deny himself and take up his cross and follow me. For whoever would save his life will lose it, but whoever loses his life for my sake will find it" (Matt. 16:24-25).

This is the point of the tale. Tom Thumb, in the role of Christ, comes upon sinful – greedy/covetous – people whom he wants to serve (Matt. 20:28). In exchange for his service he doesn't want wages, but to give blows. Why? Because he's standing in for Jesus and they're not living as Christians, they're not bearing their crosses. They're unrepentant sinners. Christ is too much for them!

The journeyman said, "Oh, but I can't make any use of you, you strike far too powerfully; what will you have for the one blow?"

He has entered an arrangement with Tom (Jesus) but doesn't want to endure the agreed upon blow (cross). Isn't that how man thinks? The Biblical Jesus is too much for the unrepentant sinner. We think He's a hard man (Matt. 25:24). What does Tom say? "I will only give you quite a small blow, that's all.' Yes, indeed, the yoke of Jesus, the cross we bear in the name of Christ, is light (Matt. 11:28-30).

The blow *only* sends us over four loads of hay. What eternal injury would we suffer if we were not in Christ?!

Likewise, the bailiff tried to back out of bearing his cross, that is, receiving his blows, because he was afraid. Isn't this exactly how we, in our sinfulness, interact with Jesus? We want Him to serve us, to be the head servant even, but we're afraid of the consequences He brings. We want the blessings of a strong man, one who can help us when we need it, but we don't want Him the way He comes, with a cross. We see this in American Christianity all the time. Christians operating with a theology of glory, thinking Jesus is there to be their head servant, and to bring them success, power, wealth, health, and their best life now. But what of the cross that Christ promised in Matthew 16?

Jesus serves us for sure (Matt. 20:28). It happens every Sunday in the Divine Service, but how many of us behave like the bailiff when the time comes to bear our crosses in the name of Jesus? We try to negotiate with the Head Servant and even offer to exchange roles with Him, saying things like, "Lord, just get me out of this mess and I'll do anything you want, I'll

The Young Giant

serve you," all the while missing the irony that in repentant faith the person who bears His cross is a servant of Christ (2 Cor. 6:4-10).

When negotiation doesn't work, as it didn't for the bailiff, we conspire to rid ourselves of the trouble Jesus and His cross bring to our lives. It was our sin that killed Jesus. It was our rejection of God and His will in our lives. The story of the young giant delivers that truth to us as we read of Tom going down into the well, in service to the sinner who has plotted to kill him by rolling a millstone up so that "he would never return to daylight." But the stone isn't enough to trap him in the earth and the giant climbs out like Jesus stepping out of the tomb.

Tom continues to serve the sinner who wants him dead, and goes to the haunted mill, a picture of Christ's descent into hell (1 Pet. 3:18-20). Consider Tom undoing the spell of the mill in light of Jesus preaching to the spirits in prison, destroying hell for all who believe, and undoing the power that death and the devil had over us. No man had ever returned from the haunted mill alive. Tom does (1 Cor. 15:20).

Tom kept his end of the arrangement. He served. He wore death around his neck, he defeated the evil stronghold. Therefore, the story concludes with the bailiff and his wife hovering about in the air, and perhaps, we're told, they're still there. They were kicked up there by the young giant. But we must not follow our first inclination and read this as retribution for all the bailiff's efforts to kill Tom and avoid his blows. This isn't the bailiff getting his comeuppance. Tom represents Christ who is merciful and loving. We have to understand their being booted skyward as a sweet reward, that which is given to those who, though in their sin they may not want to suffer the cross, nonetheless, by the grace of God have been given eternal life in heaven and have reason to rejoice in suffering (Rom. 5:3-5).

Tom and the bailiff had an arrangement, a covenant you might say, and though the bailiff proved to be unfaithful in keeping it, Tom insisted that it be kept, for the young giant (Jesus) knew it was for the bailiff's good.

As sinners we can become quite frantic in our efforts to avoid our cross and the one from whom it extends: Christ crucified, who tells us that to follow Him we must deny ourselves and take up our cross daily (Luke 9:23-24). Like the bailiff, in our sin we become seriously alarmed and beside ourselves at the thought of suffering the cross. We've been in his shoes: "He walked backwards and forwards in the room, and drops of perspiration ran down from his forehead." But the Gospel of Jesus Christ cannot be disconnected from the cross. There's no avoiding it. And Jesus knows that the cross brings eternal life in heaven, what the Grimm brothers describe as hovering in the air.

In our cowardice, to avoid temporary pain and discomfort, we're willing to forfeit eternal salvation. However, our Lord loves us too much to let that happen. Despite our efforts, He makes us worthy of Him (Matt. 10:38). After all, He didn't come to bring peace to the earth, but to go around looking to give blows, to kick us into heaven (Matt. 10:34).

The Elves, Part I

A shoemaker, by no fault of his own, had become so poor that at last he had nothing left but leather for one pair of shoes. So in the evening, he cut out the shoes which he wished to begin to make the next morning, and as he had a good conscience, he lay down quietly in his bed, commended himself to God, and fell asleep.

In the morning, after he had said his prayers, and was just going to sit down to work, the two shoes stood quite finished on his table. He was astounded, and knew not what to say to it. He took the shoes in his hands to observe them closer, and they were so neatly made that there was not one bad stitch in them, just as if they were intended as a masterpiece.

The Elves, Part I

Soon after, a buyer came in, and as the shoes pleased him so well, he paid more for them than was customary, and, with the money, the shoemaker was able to purchase leather for two pairs of shoes. He cut them out at night, and next morning was about to set to work with fresh courage; but he had no need to do so, for, when he got up, they were already made, and buyers also were not wanting, who gave him money enough to buy leather for four pairs of shoes. The following morning, too, he found the four pairs made; and so it went on constantly, what he cut out in the evening was finished by the morning, so that he soon had his honest independence again, and at last became a wealthy man.

Now it happened that one evening not long before Christmas, when the man had been cutting out, he said to his wife, before going to bed, "What would you think if we were to stay up tonight to see who it is that lends us this helping hand?"

The woman liked the idea, and lighted a candle, and then they hid themselves in a corner of the room, behind some clothes which were hanging up there, and watched. When it was midnight, two pretty little naked men came, sat down by the shoemaker's table, took all the work which was cut out before them and began to stitch, and sew, and hammer so skillfully and so quickly with their little fingers that the shoemaker could not turn away his eyes for astonishment. They did not stop until all was done, and stood finished on the table, and they ran quickly away.

The next morning the woman said, "The little men have made us rich, and we really must show that we are grateful for it. They run about so, and have nothing on, and must be cold. I'll tell you what I'll do: I will make them little shirts, and coats, and vests, and trousers, and knit both of them a pair of stockings, and you too, make them two little pairs of shoes."

The man said, "I shall be very glad to do it;" and one night, when everything was ready, they laid their presents all together on the table instead of the cut out work, and then concealed themselves to see how the little men would behave.

At midnight they came bounding in, and wanted to get to work at once, but as they did not find any leather cut out, but only the pretty little articles of clothing, they were at first astonished, and then they showed intense delight. They dressed themselves with the greatest rapidity, putting the pretty clothes on, and singing,

> *"Now we are boys so fine to see,*
> *Why should we longer cobblers be?"*

Then they danced and skipped and leapt over chairs and benches. At last they danced out of doors.

From that time on they came no more, but as long as the shoemaker lived all went well with him, and all his undertakings prospered.

* * *

IN Romans 7 the Christian learns that he isn't the one who sins, but that it's the sin within him that does the thing he doesn't want to do. "...it is no longer I who do it, but sin that dwells within me" (Rom. 7:17).

Like the brothers Grimm, one might say that the poverty of sin, when it's experienced in the life of a baptized believer, is "no fault of his own." How? Because the person who commends himself to God – as the shoemaker is said to have done – lives the Christian life of prayer. He relies on God. Living in repentant faith he trusts (despite his impoverished conditions) that God will continue to take care of him. That person's sin is no fault of his own, because it is no longer he who does it, but the sin that dwells within him.

Baptism is key. Without it a person cannot make the Romans 7 distinction, for without it it's impossible to commend one's self to God. Without it it's impossible to make the bold claim when you sin that it wasn't you, but the sin that dwells within you.

This tale is all about baptism. The baptized shoemaker, perhaps in a state of not understanding his actions, doing what he himself did not want to do, was poor (Rom. 7:15). Though he was a believer, the sin within him had finally brought him to the point where he had only enough leather for one pair of shoes.

I suspect if we knew his whole story we would see a Christian man who behaves just like Christians do today. Like I do. Like you do. I tend to rely entirely on myself to survive. To my chagrin, I only go to God when the situation becomes dire. It certainly was that for the shoemaker. When you and I finally come to rely on God, we see that He's always been there, that He already took care of everything, that He did so in our baptism.

Let me ask you, in what was the shoemaker's livelihood? In making shoes? No. His livelihood, like every believer's, is found in baptism – in Christ! It's in our being connected to Christ's life, death, and resurrection that everything is taken care of. It's there that we are surprised to find a perfect livelihood "so neatly made that there [is] not one bad stitch... just as if [it] was intended as a masterpiece." It is a masterpiece. God's masterpiece. He has done everything for you.

We see this as the story continues. With the first pair of shoes, the man is taken back to his baptism, he is reminded that his life is not in his hands, but in God's. Not only does God do all the immediate work in his (our) life, as the brothers Grimm demonstrate through the elves (angels perhaps?), but He also has done the work of ordering all of creation so that "for those who love God all things work together for good..." (Rom. 8:28). It's because of God that "a buyer came in, and as the shoes pleased him so well, he paid more for them than was customary..."

This baptismal blessing prompts us to action. It causes us to want to "set to work with fresh courage," to live out our vocations, and even then we find that God is the one still actively doing the work. More shoes for the shoemaker! This is the salvation process, it's what maturing in the faith looks like. The Gospel motivates, creating more Gospel-motivated action. All of it done by God!

"Wretched man that I am! Who will deliver me from this body of death?" (Rom. 7:24)

The answer is Christ Jesus. He delivers us from death as we are baptized in the Triune name of God. In Christ through baptism, we, like the shoemaker, have our "honest independence again," our freedom from sin, which does truly make us wealthy, for we have the treasures of heaven!

The shoemaker and his wife, having been blessed, want to show their appreciation, so, in an offering of thanksgiving they give back to those who have given them so much, and they do so out of the wealth they've acquired from them. There is no need to squabble about their seemingly misplaced appreciation. By giving to the elves, they intend to show their gratitude to

The Elves, Part I

that which is the source of their fortune, to God.

The elves receive these gifts in a way that doesn't detract from God and His generosity, but that leads me to believe they were faithful servants. They got out of the way. The shoemaker had matured. He had grown in his reliance on God through the servants the Lord had sent. He was brought to the point where joy and appreciation were pouring out of him and his household. The elves had accomplished what they were sent to do. In service to God they had brought this man back to his baptismal faith. They strengthened him in his true livelihood. Who wouldn't dance and skip and leap over chairs and benches? The elves were wearing the fruit of their labors!

"From that time forth they came no more, but as long as the shoemaker lived all went well with him, and all his undertakings prospered." He had been restored to his baptismal life! He had learned that his livelihood was in something beyond himself, something far greater than his misunderstood actions (Rom. 7:15). He was back to living a life of faith in Christ.

Remember, this is a story. Stating that "all his undertakings prospered" is the storytellers' way of communicating that the shoemaker was no longer relying on himself, but on God. It's not, as some might conclude, advocating the prosperity gospel. Not at all. Did the shoemaker go on to do the things he did not want to do (Rom. 7:15)? You bet. I do. You do. And should we meet him in his last days, once again in poverty, we could still say that "all went well with him, and all his undertakings prospered" for he was baptized and he could say,

> I myself serve the law of God with my mind, but with my flesh I serve the law of sin. There is therefore now no condemnation for those who are in Christ Jesus. For the law of the Spirit of life has set [me] free in Christ Jesus from the Law of sin and death... For those who live according to the flesh set their minds on the things of the flesh [earthly prosperity in this case], but those who live according to the Spirit set their minds on the things of the Spirit... [I], however, [am] not in the flesh but in the Spirit [because] the Spirit of God dwells in

[me as a baptized believer in Christ] (Rom. 7:25-8:2, 5, 9).

The Elves, Part II

THERE was once a poor servant girl, who was industrious and cleanly, and swept the house every day, and emptied her sweepings on the great heap in front of the door. One morning when she was just going back to her work, she found a letter on this heap, and as she could not read, she put her broom in the corner, and took the letter to her master and mistress, and behold it was an invitation from the elves, who asked the girl to hold a child for them at its christening. The girl did not know what to do, but at length, after much persuasion, and as they told her that it was not right to refuse an invitation of this kind, she consented.

Then three elves came and conducted her to a hollow mountain, where the little folks

The Elves, Part II

lived. Everything there was small, but more elegant and beautiful than can be described. The baby's mother lay in a bed of black ebony ornamented with pearls, the coverlids were embroidered with gold, the cradle was of ivory, the bath of gold.

The girl stood as godmother, and then wanted to go home again, but the little elves urgently entreated her to stay three days with them. So she stayed, and passed the time in pleasure and gaiety, and the little folks did all they could to make her happy. At last she set out on her way home. Then first they filled her pockets quite full of money, and after that they led her out of the mountain again.

When she got home, she wanted to begin her work, and took the broom, which was still standing in the corner, in her hand and began to sweep. Then some strangers came out of the house, who asked her who she was, and what business she had there? And she had not, as she thought, been three days with the little men in the mountains, but seven years, and in the meantime her former masters had died.

* * *

LIKE the three men who visited Abraham (Gen. 18:1-4), in this story three elves came to a poor servant girl. She was invited to be a baby elf's godmother. As in part one, baptism appears to be our theme. Of course it is! It was the elf child's christening that brought about the servant girl's adventure, pleasure, riches, and freedom.

We're told she was taken to a hollow mountain where everything was "more elegant and beautiful than can be described." In the context of baptism, the idea of a hollow mountain sends our minds to Christ's tomb. The Elegance and beauty of it all nudges us to what St. John saw in Revelation 21:10-11, "And he carried me away in the Spirit to a great, high *mountain,* and showed me the holy city...having the glory of God, its radiance like a most rare jewel, like jasper, clear as crystal"(emphasis mine).

Christ's three day stay in the tomb is directly connected to what John saw. It is the way to such a glorious, elegant, and beautiful place.

> ...the little elves urgently entreated her to stay three days with them. So she stayed,

The Elves, Part II

and passed the time in pleasure and gaiety... And she had not, as she thought, been three days with the little men in the mountains, but seven years...

When we're baptized into Christ we die with Him and are buried with Him. We're brought to His three-day event in a hollowed out mountain. A joyous adventure filled with pleasure and gaiety that we're urgently entreated to embark upon.

An interesting part of this story is the passing of time. The servant girl stays for three days only to find out it's been seven years. Baptism is not a one-time event that happens in our lives, but rather an ongoing reality, which is brought to completion at our death. Perhaps the completion emphasis is to be found in the number seven, the biblical number of completion or perfection. Are we not made perfect in Christ through our baptism?

Returning home she discovers her former masters have died. Through baptism we're set free. We may think of Exodus 21:2, "When you buy a Hebrew slave, he shall serve six years, and in the seventh he shall go out free, for nothing."

But let us not stop there. This whole story finds it's root in Romans 6:1-11.

> What shall we say then? Are we to continue in sin that grace may abound? By no means! How can we who died to sin still live in it? Do you not know that all of us who have been baptized into Christ Jesus were baptized into his death? We were buried therefore with him by baptism into death, in order that, just as Christ was raised from the dead by the glory of the Father, we too might walk in newness of life.
>
> For if we have been united with him in a death like his, we shall certainly be united with him in a resurrection like his. We know that our old self was crucified with him in order that the body of sin might be brought to nothing, so that we would no longer be enslaved to sin. For one who has died has been set free from sin. Now if we have died with Christ, we believe that we will also live with him. We know that Christ, being raised from the dead, will never die again; death no longer has

dominion over him. For the death he died he died to sin, once for all, but the life he lives he lives to God. So you also must consider yourselves dead to sin and alive to God in Christ Jesus.

In baptism we find pleasure and gaiety–we're given a life of elegance and beauty, indeed a complete life. The elves give the poor servant girl money. We would do well to see such a gift as the riches of heaven – forgiveness, salvation, and eternal life – that are bestowed on us in our baptism. In the now-but-not-yet reality of being a baptized believer living on this side of the resurrection, when we step away from the font we step back to a life that looks just like the one we had before our adventure into the "elf mountain" of Christ's glory. However, it most certainly is not!

The Elves, Part III

A certain mother's child had been taken away out of its cradle by the elves, and a changeling with a large head and staring eyes, which would do nothing but eat and drink, laid in its place. In her trouble she went to her neighbor, and asked her advice. The neighbor said that she was to carry the changeling into the kitchen, set it down on the hearth, light a fire, and boil some water in two eggshells, which would make the changeling laugh, and if he laughed, all would be over with him. The woman did everything that her neighbor directed her to do. When she put the egg-shells with water on the fire, the imp said,

"I am as old now as the Wester forest,

The Elves, Part III

> *but never yet have I seen
> anyone boil anything in an eggshell!"*

And he began to laugh at it. Whilst he was laughing, suddenly came a host of little elves, who brought the right child, set it down on the hearth, and took the changeling away with them.

* * *

IT'S no surprise that Baptism is the theme in part III of *The Elves*. It was the theme of parts I and II. The tale is a threefold expression of the Sacrament. One might wonder why the elves, those splendid creatures who live in the heavenly mountains (see previous chapter on part II), would take a child out of his cradle and away from his mother only to bring him back again after a changeling laid in his place. What's the point?

Isn't it obvious?

Notice the pattern: child, changeling, child. Or to state it another way: new, old, new again. Add in the care of a neighbor (Christians are called to love their neighbor, Matt. 22:36-40; Rom. 15:2; Gal. 5:13-14, 6:2), water, and the fire that boils it (Matt. 3:11), and, well, what we have is the story of Baptism.

Consider the second description of the pattern above (new, old, new again). Is this not the story of man? When God created us, He made us new creatures, created in His image, made without sin (Gen. 1:26-28). But, like a child taken away from his mother, we sinned (Gen. 3:1-7). We were removed from our cradle, from the Garden of Eden (Gen. 3:23-24) "and a changeling with a large head and staring eyes" – a sinner – took the place of God's perfect creation.

Think about this changeling for a minute. Is it not a precise description of sinful man? "A large head and staring eyes" pretty much nails it. We're big headed with the knowledge of good and evil, idolatry swelling our noggins as we long to be like God (Gen. 3:5). And how about those "staring eyes"? Oh yes indeed:

> So when the woman *saw* that the tree was good for food, and that it was a delight to the *eyes*, and that the tree was to be desired to make one wise [or shall we say big headed?], she took of its fruit and ate, and she also gave some to her husband who

was with her, and he ate. Then the *eyes* of both were opened, and they knew that they were naked... (Gen. 3:6-7). (Emphasis mine)

We all contend with this changeling, the sinner within who would gladly lay in our place, enjoying the provisions (eating and drinking) God intended for His children. Like Grimm's changeling who laughs at boiling water in eggshells and says, "I am as old now as the Wester forest," the sinner within each of us is an old man (Rom. 6:6; Eph. 2:15, 4:22; Col. 3:9). But after the waters of holy baptism, the new is restored. We're returned to how God intended us to be, each of us a child in His care (Eph. 4:23-24; Col. 3:10).

Child, changeling, child. We're created in God's image, His children. Then because of sin we're changed into something else, an imposter masquerading as a child. But God, through Baptism into Christ, ends the time of the old changeling, just like the neighbor said, "all would be over with him" as we, the children of God, are restored to our rightful place, "set down on the hearth," home once again.

Fair Katrinelje and Pif-Paf-Poltrie

"GOOD-DAY, Father Hollenthe."

"Many thanks, Pif-paf-poltrie."

"May I be allowed to have your daughter?"

"Oh, yes, if Mother Malcho (Milch-cow), Brother High-and-Mighty, Sister Käsetraut, and fair Katrinelje are willing, you can have her."

"Where is Mother Malcho, then?"

"She is in the cow-house, milking the cow."

"Goodday, Mother Malcho."

"Many thanks, Pif-paf-poltrie."

"May I be allowed to have your daughter?"

"Oh, yes, if Father Hollenthe, Brother High-and-Mighty, Sister Käsetraut, and fair Katrinelje are willing, you can have her."

Fair Katrinelje and Pif-Paf-Poltrie

"Where is Brother High-and-Mighty, then?"

"He is in the room chopping some wood."

"Good-day, Brother High-and-Mighty."

"Many thanks, Pif-paf-poltrie."

"May I be allowed to have your sister?"

"Oh, yes, if Father Hollenthe, Mother Malcho, Sister Käsetraut, and fair Katrinelje are willing, you can have her."

"Where is Sister Käsetraut, then?"

"She is in the garden cutting cabbages."

"Good-day, sister Käsetraut."

"Many thanks, Pif-paf-poltrie."

"May I be allowed to have your sister?"

"Oh, yes, if Father Hollenthe, Mother Malcho, Brother High-and- Mighty, and fair Katrinelje are willing, you may have her."

"Where is fair Katrinelje, then?"

"She is in the room counting out her farthings." "Good-day, fair Katrinelje."

"Many thanks, Pif-paf-poltrie."

"Will you be my bride?"

"Oh, yes, if Father Hollenthe, Mother Malcho, Brother High-and-Mighty, and Sister Käsetraut are willing, I am ready."

"Fair Katrinelje, how much dowry do you have?"

"Fourteen farthings in ready money, three and a half groschen owing to me, half a pound of dried apples, a handful of fried bread, and a handful of spices.

"And many other things are mine,
Have I not a dowry fine?"

"Pif-paf-poltrie, what is your trade? Are you a tailor?"
"Something better."
"A shoemaker?"
"Something better."
"A husbandman?"
"Something better."
"A joiner?"
"Something better."
"A smith?"
"Something better."
"A miller?"
"Something better."
"Perhaps a broom maker?"
"Yes, that's what I am, is it not a fine trade?"

* * *

Fair Katrinelje and Pif-Paf-Poltrie

NAMES, names, names. What fun! But what work. All these curious names. Names like Mother Malcho and Pif-Paf-Poltrie. Oh, and the ever informative name of Brother High-and-Mighty. Everyone in the family is called something superb, at least to my eyes. Father Hollenthe, Sister Käsetraut, and of course, fair Katrinelje.

The progression of the story puts these names front and center by repeating them over and over again, making the story that much more fun, and that much more challenging to read, especially aloud. But what of the actual story? Where do we find God's Word in this tale?

To answer that we must ask ourselves, what's the story about? A suitor, Pif-Paf-Poltrie, seeking the hand of his bride, fair Katrinelje, right? That's it. That's the whole story. In this simple plot the Christian sees a picture of Christ and His bride, the Church. Like Christ, Pif-Paf-Poltrie didn't simply walk up to His bride and ask her to marry Him. It wasn't as easy as that. The betrothal wasn't without trial.

In order to win His bride, our Lord obeyed the will of God perfectly, which led to the grueling experience of dying on the cross (Is.

53:5). He earned her hand. Likewise, Pif-Paf-Poltrie did as was proper and obeyed the will of Father Hollenthe, in order to win Katrinelje's hand.

It's a pleasant misery that the reader endures as he walks through this story, for the difficulty Pif-Paf-Poltrie endured is subjected upon you and me in the tiresome reading of each name over and over and over again. The Grimm brothers don't spare us a single syllable. There's no reprieve for the weary reader. Every name is declared in its entirety each time our humble broom maker asks to have Katrinelje, as he obeys her father's law.

Through this literary technique, we're brought into Pif-Paf-Poltrie's labor to experience something similar to what he endured in order to have his bride. In this way, we come to understand something of the theology of the cross, as we take up our cross and follow Pif-Paf-Poltrie, who suffered in order that we might know Christ and Him crucified.

What's more, all this work is put forward to gain a wife who brings nothing to the marriage, though, to be fair, she would like to think she does. Christ went to the cross to earn for

Himself a bride who has nothing to offer Him (Rom. 5:8).

To this, one might say, "But with such a worthless dowry she's a right fit for a humble man with a trade such as broom making."

Dear reader, trouble yourself to see the truth. Katrinelje and Pif-Paf-Poltrie are not of the same lowly estate.

In this story Katrinelje stands in for the Bride of Christ (sainted sinners who can do no good on our own). Pif-Paf-Poltrie's trade, however, is truly "something better" than all those she lists. We see this throughout the Gospels; she, like the disciples, is used to thinking in earthly terms. When Christ came the Jews were expecting an earthly king to restore the glory of Israel. But, Pif-Paf-Poltrie, in his humility, is the servant of servants (Christ) as he makes the tools servants use to carry out the work of cleaning. Katrinelje would've liked him to be a tailor, shoemaker, husbandman, joiner, smith, or miller, but he was "something better." Christ is "something better" than an earthly king. He's "something better." He's a broom maker! The servant of all servants!

The Old Beggar Woman

THERE was once an old woman, but you have surely seen an old woman go a-begging before now? This woman begged likewise, and when she got anything she said, "May God reward you."

The beggar woman came to a door, and there by the fire a friendly rogue of a boy was standing warming himself. The boy said kindly to the poor old woman as she was standing shivering thus by the door, "Come, old mother, and warm yourself."

She came in, but stood too near the fire, so that her old rags began to burn, and she was not aware of it. The boy stood and saw that, but he ought to have put the flames out. Is it not true that he ought to have put them out? And if he had not any water, then should he have wept all the water in his body out of his eyes, and that would have supplied two pretty streams with which to extinguish them.

* * *

"MAY God reward you." The blessing of the old beggar woman in this story. She spoke these words to those who gave her something when she asked. These four words call to mind what our Lord Jesus said, "It is more blessed to give than to receive" (Acts 20:35). She received something, but she gave as well. She blessed those who showed her love. But of course, this is not where our focus is drawn. This brief story is centered on the poor behavior of the "friendly rogue of a boy" who at first appears to be concerned with serving his neighbor, but who is ultimately shown to be not at all interested in the welfare of the woman.

> She came in, but stood too near the fire, so that her old rags began to burn, and she was not aware of it. The boy stood and saw that, but he ought to have put the flames

out. Is it not true that he ought to have put them out?

Yes, it is true that he ought to have put them out. How often do we see someone in need and yet we don't help them? Is it not true that we ought to put out the "flames" that are consuming our neighbor when we see them?
Indeed!
Loving our neighbor as ourselves (Matt. 22:39) is not done in word and talk only, but in deed and truth (1 John 3:18). It's easy for anyone, friendly rogue or otherwise, to say "Come... warm yourself," but the Christian is called to more than empty words. We deceive ourselves if we think our faith is expressed in hollow gestures. Christ is the Word of God incarnate, likewise the words of the Christian are realized in deed and truth for the good of our neighbor.

> What good is it, my brothers, if someone says he has faith but does not have works? Can that faith save him? If a brother or sister is poorly clothed and lacking in daily food, and one of you says to them, "Go in peace, be warmed and filled," without

giving them the things needed for the body, what good is that? So also faith by itself, if it does not have works, is dead (James 2:14-17).

The story's conclusion is hyperbolic, showing just how far a person should be willing to go in service to neighbor. The boy "should have wept all the water in his body out of his eyes..." Is it not true that this is precisely the love we should have for others? We don't, but we should. Is it not true, however, that this is precisely the love Jesus has for us? If crying was what He needed to do to save us from the flames, He would have cried and cried and cried some more.

As it is, crying isn't how He came upon water to save us. Apart from all exaggeration, dying was what was necessary to show God's love for us. Dying on the cross where He was pierced for our transgressions, where two streams (blood and water–Communion and Baptism) flowed (John 19:34), extinguishing the fires of hell so that we would live.

The Jew Among Thorns

THERE was once a rich man, who had a servant who served him diligently and honestly: he was every morning the first out of bed, and the last to go to rest at night; and, whenever there was a difficult job to be done, which nobody cared to undertake, he was always the first to set himself to it. Moreover, he never complained, but was contented with everything, and always merry.

When a year was ended, his master gave him no wages, for he said to himself, "That is the cleverest way; for I shall save something, and he will not go away, but stay quietly in my service. The servant said nothing, but did his work the second year as he had done it the first; and when at the end of this, likewise, he

The Jew Among Thorns

received no wages, he made himself happy, and still stayed on.

When the third year also was past, the master considered, put his hand in his pocket, but pulled nothing out. Then at last the servant said, "Master, for three years I have served you honestly, be so good as to give me what I ought to have, for I wish to leave, and look about me a little more in the world."

"Yes, my good fellow," answered the old miser; "you have served me industriously, and, therefore, you shall be cheerfully rewarded;" And he put his hand into his pocket, but counted out only three farthings, saying, "There, you have a farthing for each year; that is large and liberal pay, such as you would have received from few masters."

The honest servant, who understood little about money, put his fortune into his pocket, and thought, "Ah! now that I have my purse full, why need I trouble and plague myself any longer with hard work!" So on he went, up hill and down dale; and sang and jumped to his heart's content.

Now it came to pass that as he was going by a thicket a little man stepped out, and called to him, "Whither away, merry brother? I see you do not carry many cares."

"Why should I be sad?" answered the servant; "I have enough; three years' wages are jingling in my pocket."

"How much is your treasure?" the dwarf asked him.

"How much? Three farthings sterling, all told."

"Look here," said the dwarf, "I am a poor needy man, give me your three farthings; I can work no longer, but you are young, and can easily earn your bread."

And as the servant had a good heart, and felt pity for the old man, he gave him the three farthings, saying, "Take them in the name of Heaven, I shall not be any the worse for it."

Then the little man said, "As I see you have a good heart I grant you three wishes, one for each farthing, they shall all be fulfilled."

"Aha?" said the servant, "you are one of those who can work wonders! Well, then, if it is to be so, I wish, first, for a gun, which shall hit everything that I aim at; secondly, for a fiddle, which when I play on it, shall compel all who hear it to dance; thirdly, that if I ask a favor of any one he shall not be able to refuse it."

The Jew Among Thorns

"All that shall you have," said the dwarf; and put his hand into the bush, and only think, there lay a fiddle and gun, all ready, just as if they had been ordered. These he gave to the servant, and then said to him, "Whatever you may ask at any time, no man in the world shall be able to deny you."

"Heart alive! What can one desire more?" said the servant to himself, and went merrily onwards.

Soon afterwards he met a Jew with a long goat's beard, who was standing listening to the song of a bird which was sitting up at the top of a tree. "Good heavens," he was exclaiming, "that such a small creature should have such a fearfully loud voice! If it were but mine! If only someone would sprinkle some salt upon its tail!"

"If that is all," said the servant, "the bird shall soon be down here;" And taking aim he pulled the trigger, and down fell the bird into the thorn bushes. "Go, you rogue," he said to the Jew, "and fetch the bird out for yourself!"

"Oh!" said the Jew, "Leave out the rogue, my master, and I will do it at once. I will get the bird out for myself, as you really have hit it."

Then he lay down on the ground, and began to crawl into the thicket.

When he was fast among the thorns, the good servant's humor so tempted him that he took up his fiddle and began to play. In a moment the Jew's legs began to move, and to jump into the air, and the more the servant fiddled the better went the dance.

But the thorns tore his shabby coat from him, combed his beard, and pricked and plucked him all over the body. "Oh dear," cried the Jew, "what do I want with your fiddling? Leave the fiddle alone, master; I do not want to dance."

But the servant did not listen to him, and thought, "You have fleeced people often enough, now the thorn bushes shall do the same to you;" and he began to play over again, so that the Jew had to jump higher than ever, and scraps of his coat were left hanging on the thorns.

"Oh, woe's me!" cried the Jew; "I will give the gentleman whatsoever he asks if only he leaves off fiddling a purse full of gold."

"If you are so liberal," said the servant, "I will stop my music; but this I must say to your credit, that you dance to it so well that it is

The Jew Among Thorns

quite an art;" and having taken the purse he went his way.

The Jew stood still and watched the servant quietly until he was far off and out of sight, and then he screamed out with all his might, "You miserable musician, you beer-house fiddler! Wait till I catch you alone, I will hunt you till the soles of your shoes fall off! You ragamuffin! Just put five farthings in your mouth, and then you may be worth three halfpence!" and went on abusing him as fast as he could speak. As soon as he had refreshed himself a little in this way, and got his breath again, he ran into the town to the justice.

"My lord judge," he said, "I have come to make a complaint; see how a rascal has robbed and ill-treated me on the public highway! A stone on the ground might pity me; my clothes all torn, my body pricked and scratched, my little all gone with my purse, good ducats, each piece better than the last; for God's sake let the man be thrown into prison!"

"Was it a soldier," said the judge, "who cut you so with his sabre?"

"Nothing of the sort!" said the Jew; "It was no sword that he had, but a gun hanging at his back, and a fiddle at his neck; the wretch may easily be known."

So the judge sent his people out after the man, and they found the good servant, who had been going quite slowly along, and they found, too, the purse with the money upon him. As soon as he was taken before the judge he said, "I did not touch the Jew, nor take his money; he gave it to me of his own free will, that I might leave off fiddling because he could not bear my music."

"Heaven defend us!" cried the Jew, "His lies are as thick as flies upon the wall."

But the judge also did not believe his tale, and said, "This is a bad defense, no Jew would do that." And because he had committed robbery on the public highway, he sentenced the good servant to be hanged.

As he was being led away the Jew again screamed after him, "You vagabond! You dog of a fiddler! Now you are going to receive your well-earned reward!"

The servant walked quietly with the hangman up the ladder, but upon the last step he turned around and said to the judge, "Grant me just one request before I die."

The Jew Among Thorns

"Yes, if you do not ask your life," said the judge.

"I do not ask for life," answered the servant, "but as a last favor let me play once more upon my fiddle."

The Jew raised a great cry of "Murder! Murder! For goodness' sake do not allow it! Do not allow it!"

But the judge said, "Why should I not let him have this short pleasure? It has been granted to him, and he shall have it." However, he could not have refused on account of the gift which had been bestowed on the servant.

Then the Jew cried, "Oh! Woe's me! Tie me, tie me fast!" while the good servant took his fiddle from his neck, and made ready.

As he gave the first scrape, they all began to quiver and shake, the judge, his clerk, and the hangman and his men, and the cord fell out of the hand of the one who was going to tie the Jew fast. At the second scrape all raised their legs, and the hangman let go his hold of the good servant, and made himself ready to dance. At the third scrape they all leaped up and began to dance; the judge and the Jew being the best at jumping. Soon all who had gathered in the marketplace out of curiosity were dancing with them; old and young, fat and lean, one with another. The dogs, likewise, which had run there got up on their hind legs and capered about; and the longer he played, the higher sprang the dancers, so that they knocked against each other's heads, and began to shriek terribly.

At length the judge cried, quite out of breath, "I will give you your life if you will only stop fiddling."

The good servant thereupon had compassion, took his fiddle and hung it around his neck again, and stepped down the ladder. Then he went up to the Jew, who was lying upon the ground panting for breath, and said, "You rascal, now confess, where you got the money, or I will take my fiddle and begin to play again."

"I stole it, I stole it!" he cried; "But you have earned it honestly."

So the judge had the Jew taken to the gallows and hanged as a thief.

* * *

WHAT happens to the unrepentant sinner? What happens to those who've been given

God's Word, but reject the truth, who continue in their wicked ways and set themselves against the Lord? That's what this story is about.

The good servant, who, like Christ, finds himself at the gallows after three years of faithful service, is placed in contrast with a Jewish rogue who goes to a judge in order to deal with the man he believes has wronged him. Just like our Savior, the good servant is sentenced to death; however, unlike the Lord, in the end he lives while the Jew is hanged as a thief. While Jesus has died for the whole world, some personally deny the gift of His death. These people are like the Jew among the thorns, a thief to be hanged, a rogue without the good servant's death to save them from their own.

In a narrow sense one can see how this is the story of Jesus (the Good Servant) and the pharisaical Jews, those rogues who sought to have Pontius Pilate judge the man they accused of breaking God's Law when in reality they were the ones who had robbed the Jewish people of their treasure–God's Word.

In a broader sense this story is of anyone who knows the truth – that he is a sinner – yet denies it, thereby accusing God of wrongdoing (1 John 1:10). Such a person must face the penalty of his sins alone. He chooses to offer a sacrifice to atone for his sin based on his own merit. Such a person quickly finds that the penalty for his sin is death. He could've been Isaac, saved from his father's blade, but instead he chose for himself to be the ram caught in the thorn bush (Gen. 22:13). Isaac was saved from death, likewise the Christian. Not the unbeliever, not the unrepentant.

Who wants to be "a [an unbeliever] with a long goat's beard" caught in a thorn bush? Who wants to be hanged as a thief (on a cross) when Jesus has offered Himself as our substitute? He's our scapegoat so we don't have to be a ram, or a goat, long bearded or otherwise.

The unbelieving heart of the Jew is revealed when he rejects what the good servant calls him–rogue–just before he ends up caught in the thorns.

"Go, you *rogue*" he said to the Jew... "Oh! said the Jew, "Leave out the *rogue*, my master, and I will do it at once..." (emphasis mine)

In light of John 12:48 it's a brilliant foreshadowing of the conclusion. "The one who rejects me and does not receive my words has a judge; the word that I have spoken will judge him on the last day."

The unbeliever doesn't want the substitutionary atonement of Jesus Christ. He wants the historical Jesus locked up, put out of the way, and punished for exposing his sin and mistreating him in his waywardness, right? Is that not what the Jew in our story requests of the judge? "Let the man be thrown in prison!" He doesn't want Jesus to die, for that would mean salvation! He wants Jesus punished, because Jesus highlights his sinfulness. After all, Jesus is "a stumbling block to Jews and foolishness to Gentiles" (1 Cor. 1:23).

The end of the story presents a stern warning to all unbelievers as the Jew is forced to confess his guilt, that he is indeed a rogue, a sinner! In repentant faith the Christian confesses his sins now, he hears the Word of God call him a rogue – a sinner – and he acknowledges the truth; the unbeliever, however, doesn't receive God's Word and will confess his sins before the judge on Judgment Day. Either way, "every tongue shall confess to God" (Rom. 14:11).

To confess our sins today is to have life through the Good Servant, Jesus, who died the death of a thief on a cross that we would be saved. To confess our sins on Judgement Day is to reject Christ's death and be taken to the gallows and hanged as thieves.

King Thrushbeard

A King had a daughter who was beautiful beyond all measure, but so proud and haughty withal that no suitor was good enough for her. She sent away one after the other, and ridiculed them as well.

Once the King made a great feast and invited, from far and near, all the young men likely to marry. They were all marshalled in a row according to their rank and standing; first came the kings, then the grand-dukes, then the princes, the earls, the barons, and the gentry. Then the King's daughter was led through the ranks, but to every one she had some objection to make; one was too fat, "The wine cask," she said. Another was too tall, "Long and thin has little in." The third was too short, "Short and thick is never quick." The fourth was too pale, "As pale as death." The fifth too red, "A fighting cock." The sixth was not straight enough, "A green log dried behind the stove."

So she had something to say against every one, but she made herself especially merry over a good king who stood quite high up in the row, and whose chin had grown a little crooked. "Well," she cried and laughed, "he has a chin like a thrush's beak!" and from that time he got the name of King Thrushbeard.

But the old King, when he saw that his daughter did nothing but mock the people, and despised all the suitors who were gathered there, was very angry, and swore that she should have for her husband the very first beggar that came to his doors.

A few days afterwards a fiddler came and sang beneath the windows, trying to earn a small alms. When the King heard him he said, "Let him come up." So the fiddler came in, in his dirty, ragged clothes, and sang before the King and his daughter, and when he had ended he asked for a trifling gift. The King said, "Your song has pleased me so well that I will give you my daughter there, to wife."

King Thrushbeard

The King's daughter shuddered, but the King said, "I have taken an oath to give you to the very first beggar-man, and I will keep it."

All she could say was in vain; the priest was brought, and she had to let herself be wedded to the fiddler on the spot. When that was done the King said, "Now it is not proper for you, a beggar-woman, to stay any longer in my palace, you may just go away with your husband."

The beggar-man led her out by the hand, and she was obliged to walk away on foot with him. When they came to a large forest she asked, "To whom does that beautiful forest belong?"

"It belongs to King Thrushbeard; if you had taken him, it would have been yours."

"Ah, unhappy girl that I am, if I had but taken King Thrushbeard!"

Afterwards they came to a meadow, and she asked again, "To whom does this beautiful green meadow belong?"

"It belongs to King Thrushbeard; if you had taken him, it would have been yours."

"Ah, unhappy girl that I am, if I had but taken King Thrushbeard!"

Then they came to a large town, and she asked again, "To whom does this fine large town belong?"

"It belongs to King Thrushbeard; if you had taken him, it would have been yours."

"Ah, unhappy girl that I am, if I had but taken King Thrushbeard!"

"It does not please me," said the fiddler, "to hear you always wishing for another husband; am I not good enough for you?"

At last they came to a very little hut, and she said, "Oh goodness! what a small house; to whom does this miserable, mean hovel belong?"

The fiddler answered, "That is my house and yours, where we shall live together."

She had to stoop in order to go in at the low door. "Where are the servants?" said the King's daughter.

"What servants?" answered the beggarman; "you must yourself do what you wish to have done. Just make a fire at once, and set on water to cook my supper, I am quite tired."

But the King's daughter knew nothing about lighting fires or cooking, and the beggarman had to lend a hand himself to get anything fairly done.

King Thrushbeard

When they had finished their scanty meal they went to bed; but he forced her to get up quite early in the morning in order to look after the house.

For a few days they lived in this way as well as might be, and came to the end of all their provisions. Then the man said, "Wife, we cannot go on any longer eating and drinking here and earning nothing. You must weave baskets."

He went out, cut some willows, and brought them home. Then she began to weave, but the tough willows wounded her delicate hands.

"I see that this will not do," said the man; "you had better spin, perhaps you can do that better."

She sat down and tried to spin, but the hard thread soon cut her soft fingers so that the blood ran down.

"See," said the man, "you are fit for no sort of work; I have made a bad bargain with you. Now I will try to make a business with pots and earthenware; you must sit in the marketplace and sell the ware."

"Alas," she thought, "if any of the people from my father's kingdom come to the market and see me sitting there, selling, how they will mock me?" But it was of no use, she had to yield unless she chose to die of hunger.

For the first time she succeeded well, for the people were glad to buy the woman's wares because she was good looking, and they paid her what she asked; many even gave her the money and left the pots with her as well. So they lived on what she had earned as long as it lasted, then the husband bought a lot of new crockery. With this she sat down at the corner of the marketplace, and set it out round about her ready for sale. But suddenly there came a drunken hussar galloping along, and he rode right among the pots so that they were all broken into a thousand bits. She began to weep, and did now know what to do for fear. "Alas! What will happen to me?" she cried; "What will my husband say to this?"

She ran home and told him of the misfortune.

"Who would seat herself at a corner of the marketplace with crockery?" said the man; "Leave off crying, I see very well that you cannot do any ordinary work, so I have been to our King's palace and have asked whether they cannot find a place for a kitchen maid, and they

King Thrushbeard

have promised me to take you; in that way you will get your food for nothing."

The King's daughter was now a kitchen maid, and had to be at the cook's beck and call, and do the dirtiest work. In both her pockets she fastened a little jar, in which she took home her share of the leavings, and upon this they lived.

It happened that the wedding of the King's eldest son was to be celebrated, so the poor woman went up and placed herself by the door of the hall to look on. When all the candles were lit, and people, each more beautiful than the other, entered, and all was full of pomp and splendor, she thought of her lot with a sad heart, and cursed the pride and haughtiness which had humbled her and brought her to so great poverty.

The smell of the delicious dishes which were being taken in and out reached her, and now and then the servants threw her a few morsels of them: these she put in her jars to take home.

All at once the King's son entered, clothed in velvet and silk, with gold chains about his neck. And when he saw the beautiful woman standing by the door he seized her by the hand,

and would have danced with her; but she refused and shrank with fear, for she saw that it was King Thrushbeard, her suitor whom she had driven away with scorn. Her struggles were of no avail, he drew her into the hall; but the string by which her pockets were hung broke, the pots fell down, the soup ran out, and the scraps were scattered all about. And when the people saw it, there arose general laughter and derision, and she was so ashamed that she would rather have been a thousand fathoms below the ground.

She sprang to the door and would have run away, but on the stairs a man caught her and brought her back; and when she looked at him it was King Thrushbeard again.

He said to her kindly, "Do not be afraid, I and the fiddler who has been living with you in that wretched hovel are one. For love of you I disguised myself so; and I also was the hussar who rode through your crockery. This was all done to humble your proud spirit, and to punish you for the insolence with which you mocked me."

Then she wept bitterly and said, "I have done great wrong, and am not worthy to be your wife."

But he said, "Be comforted, the evil days are past; now we will celebrate our wedding."

Then the maids-in-waiting came and put on her the most splendid clothing, and her father and his whole court came and wished her happiness in her marriage with King Thrushbeard, and the joy now began in earnest. I wish you and I had been there too.

* * *

WHAT sort of suitor would continue to pursue a bride who mocked him? A man full of patience and love, as we shall see. King Thrushbeard is so named because his would-be bride laughed at him upon seeing his face and cried, "he has a chin like a thrush's beak!" just as Isaiah writes concerning Jesus, "he had no form or majesty that we should look at him, and no beauty that we should desire him" (Is. 53:2b).

No matter. King Thrushbeard was not deterred by his beloved's sin – pride, haughtiness, and mockery. With a self-sacrificial plan to turn her from her great wrongs, he set aside all his kingly glory choosing to live as a beggar in order to take her hand in marriage (Phil. 2:4-11).

We mustn't make light of what it meant for King Thrushbeard to live in poverty, for this is the very picture of the incarnation of Jesus Christ, our King, who humbled Himself to serve us, His bride. (1 Tim. 6:15; Rev. 19:16; John 12:15; Matt. 20:28). And how did our Lord serve us? By sacrificing Himself so that we would turn from our sin and believe in Him.

We're shown the extent of Thrushbeard's riches as he, in the form of a beggar-man, took his beautiful bride to live with him in his home. They came upon a large forest, a beautiful green meadow, and a large town. All of which could have been the bride's if she had married King Thrushbeard, that is, if she hadn't been such an insolent sinner. He could have taken her to live in the large town, for it really was his, but instead the couple went to live in a "very little hut." The hut was of such lowly estate that when the bride saw it she exclaimed, "Oh goodness! what a small house; to whom does this miserable, mean hovel belong?" Little did she know King Thrushbeard had a reason for his actions.

> For you know the grace of our Lord Jesus Christ, that though He was rich, yet for

your sakes He became poor, so that you through His poverty might become rich (2 Cor. 8:9).

And so we see by the end of our story that that's exactly what happened to the beautiful bride who learned that her husband was actually King Thrushbeard. She received the grace of a king who was rich, yet for her sake became poor, so that she, through his poverty, might become rich – far richer than having large forests, beautiful green meadows, and large towns: rich in spirit!

But before she confessed her sin and said, "I have done great wrong, and am not worthy to be your wife," and before she was absolved of her sin with the words of her bridegroom, "Be comforted, the evil days are past; now we will celebrate our wedding," the beautiful bride settled into her new life with her still impoverished husband. As she does the reader is blessed with a series of Biblical truths.

She asked about having servants and received the reply, "you must yourself do what you wish to have done." She was not use to having to do anything for herself, she was a princess, after all.

This won't do. Not for Thrushbeard in our story, nor for Christ in reality.

In the historic Christian Church believers confess the words of the Apostles' Creed. We say, "*I* believe in God..." We don't say, "*We* believe." It's personal. *I* believe. Why? Because "the righteous [person] shall live by *his* faith" (Hab. 2:4). For more on this, take a look at Matthew 25:1-13 and Luke 7:50. But lest we're tempted to think our faith is a work we do to earn salvation, the story continues, most appropriately, with more truth.

After he saw how poorly his wife worked (she couldn't possibly save herself), the beggar-man declared, "You are fit for no sort of work." Like the bride, sinful man is unable to do anything to contribute to our salvation. God must do everything for us, hence the beggar-man saw that his bride's attempts to work failed and said, "Now *I* will try..."

The results of his efforts seat his bride in the marketplace to sell the ware. We can easily see that this is the Church seated in a passive posture, doing nothing in the marketplace of religion. Christ has done everything. We simply sit and sell the goods of Christ's efforts, that is, we proclaim the Gospel to the world. Of course, the price tag says, "free."

"For the first time she succeeded well, for the people were glad to buy the woman's wares because she was good looking." It's no wonder she succeeded for the first time. It was her bridegroom's plan. As history has shown, many people have come to believe in Jesus, to "buy" the Church's "wares"–the Gospel–because Christ's Bride is attractive. How many people have been drawn to the Lord's goods (forgiveness, salvation, and life everlasting) through the Church's adornment, her art and ornamentation, a sanctuary's splendid architecture, or the liturgical order of the beautiful Divine Service? The Church is attractive and indeed she draws people in by her good looks.

This, like her other attempts, however is tainted by her failure. Like the bride, we Christians continue to struggle with our failure. On our own we can do nothing well. We need our King. And when Christ returns in His glory, we will experience what she did. The bride was reunited with King Thrushbeard who came in pomp and splendor, "clothed in velvet and silk, with gold chains about his neck." While she is cursed "her pride and haughtiness which humbled her and brought her to so great poverty," the king seized her hand. She pulled away (like God's people do), and he chased after (like God always does).

Confession. Absolution. And all is well. The King and his Bride live in happiness, and joy is carried on in earnest.

As for this reader, I love how the Grimm Brothers end the tale. "I wish you and I had been there too." Amen! Would that everyone could be at the marriage feast of the Lamb. Would that everyone would curse their pride and haughtiness and be humbled and brought into poverty, "for you know the grace of our Lord Jesus Christ, that though He was rich, yet for your sakes He became poor, so that you through His poverty might become rich" (2 Cor. 8:9).

Fitcher's Bird

THERE was once a wizard who used to take the form of a poor man, and went to houses and begged, and caught pretty girls. No one knew where he carried them, for they were never seen anymore. One day he appeared before the door of a man who had three pretty daughters; he looked like a poor weak beggar, and carried a basket on his back, as if he meant to collect charitable gifts in it. He begged for a little food, and when the eldest daughter came out and was just reaching him a piece of bread, he did but touch her, and she was forced to jump into his basket. After that he hurried away with long strides, and carried her away into a dark forest to his house, which stood in the midst of it.

Everything in the house was magnificent; he gave her whatsoever she could possibly desire, and said, "My darling, you will certainly be happy with me, for you have everything your heart can wish for."

This lasted a few days, and then he said, "I must journey on, and leave you alone for a short time; there are the keys of the house; you may go everywhere and look at everything except into one room, which this little key here opens, and there I forbid you to go on pain of death." He likewise gave her an egg and said, "Preserve the egg carefully for me, and carry it continually about with you, for a great misfortune would arise from the loss of it."

She took the keys and the egg, and promised to obey him in everything. When he was gone, she went all around the house from the bottom to the top, and examined everything. The rooms shone with silver and gold, and she thought she had never seen such great splendor.

At length she came to the forbidden door; she wished to pass it by, but curiosity let her have no rest. She examined the key, it looked just like any other; she put it in the keyhole and turned it a little, and the door sprang open. But

Fitcher's Bird

what did she see when she went in? A great bloody basin stood in the middle of the room, and therein lay human beings, dead and hewn to pieces, and hard by was a block of wood, and a gleaming axe lay upon it. She was so terribly alarmed that the egg which she held in her hand fell into the basin. She got it out and washed the blood off, but in vain, it appeared again in a moment. She washed and scrubbed, but she could not get it out.

It was not long before the man came back from his journey, and the first things which he asked for were the key and the egg. She gave them to him, but she trembled as she did so, and he saw at once by the red spots that she had been in the bloody chamber. "Since you have gone into the room against my will," said he, "you shall go back into it against your own. Your life is ended." He threw her down, dragged her there by her hair, cut her head off on the block, and hewed her in pieces so that her blood ran on the ground. Then he threw her into the basin with the rest.

"Now I will fetch myself the second," said the wizard, and again he went to the house in the shape of a poor man, and begged. Then the second daughter brought him a piece of bread;

he caught her like the first, by simply touching her, and carried her away. She did not fare better than her sister. She allowed herself to be led away by her curiosity, opened the door of the bloody chamber, looked in, and had to atone for it with her life on the wizard's return.

Then he went and brought the third sister, but she was clever and crafty. When he had given her the keys and the egg, and had left her, she first put the egg away with great care, and then she examined the house, and at last went into the forbidden room. Alas, what did she behold! Both her sisters lay there in the basin, cruelly murdered, and cut in pieces. But she began to gather their limbs together and put them in order, head, body, arms and legs. And when nothing further was wanting the limbs began to move and unite themselves together, and both the maidens opened their eyes and were once more alive. Then they rejoiced and kissed and caressed each other.

On his arrival, the man at once demanded the keys and the egg, and as he could perceive no trace of any blood on it, he said, "You have stood the test, You shall be my bride." He now had no longer any power over her, and was forced to do whatsoever she desired.

Fitcher's Bird

"Oh, very well," she said, "you shall first take a basketful of gold to my father and mother, and carry it yourself on your back; in the meantime I will prepare for the wedding."

Then she ran to her sisters, whom she had hidden in a little chamber, and said, "The moment has come when I can save you. The wretch shall himself carry you home again, but as soon as you are at home send help to me." She put both of them in a basket and covered them quite over with gold, so that nothing of them was to be seen, then she called in the wizard and said to him, "Now carry the basket away, but I shall look through my little window and watch to see if you stop on the way to stand or to rest."

The wizard raised the basket on his back and went away with it, but it weighed him down so heavily that the perspiration streamed from his face. Then he sat down and wanted to rest awhile, but immediately one of the girls in the basket cried, "I am looking through my little window, and I see that you are resting. Will you go on at once?" He thought it was his bride who was calling that to him; and got up on his legs again. Once more he was going to sit down, but instantly she cried, "I am looking through my little window, and I see that you are resting. Will you go on directly?" And whenever he stood still, she cried this, and then he was forced to go onwards, until at last, groaning and out of breath, he took the basket with the gold and the two maidens into their parents' house.

At home, however, the bride prepared the marriage feast, and sent invitations to the friends of the wizard. Then she took a skull with grinning teeth, put some ornaments on it and a wreath of flowers, carried it upstairs to the garret window, and let it look out from there. When all was ready, she got into a barrel of honey, and then cut the feather bed open and rolled herself in it, until she looked like a wondrous bird, and no one could recognize her. Then she went out of the house, and on her way she met some of the wedding guests, who asked,

"O, Fitcher's bird, why come here?"

"I come from Fitcher's house quite near."

"And what may the young bride be doing?"

*"From cellar to garret she's swept all clean,
And now from the window she's peeping, I ween."*

At last she met the bridegroom, who was coming slowly back. He, like the others, asked,

"O, Fitcher's bird, why come here?"

"I come from Fitcher's house quite near."

"And what may the young bride be doing?

*"From cellar to garret she's swept all clean,
And now from the window she's peeping, I ween."*

The bridegroom looked up, saw the decked out skull, thought it was his bride, and nodded to her, greeting her kindly. But when he and his guests had all gone into the house, the brothers and kinsmen of the bride, who had been sent to rescue her, arrived. They locked all the doors of the house, that no one might escape, set fire to it, and the wizard and all his crew had to burn.

* * *

WE'VE seen the wedding theme before in the Brothers' tales, such as in our last story, King Thrushbeard. The theme delivers a royal wedding and a happy ending that points us to Christ and His Bride, the Church. In this tale, however, we're exposed to what we might consider an anti-king, and the bride preparing for an anti-wedding, indeed we see the picture of an anti-Christ. But in keeping with the truth of Scripture we're delighted to learn that the Bride isn't wed to her evil captor, instead she's given the power, through the blood of Christ, to overcome him and even given a part in bringing about his destruction in the proclamation of the Gospel (Rev. 12:11).

"There once was a wizard" whose house stood in the midst of a dark forest. Make no mistake, this is not the fictional wizards we love to celebrate. We're not dealing with Tolkien's Gandalf or Rowling's Harry Potter. No, dear reader, we have before us a wicked wizard who dwells in the midst of darkness. A characterization of Satan.

We've encountered the dark forest before, haven't we? (see *The Frog-King* chapter) It's our fallen world, God's good creation shrouded in darkness. Now, here we are in the middle of it. What should we expect to find in such a sin-filled place, but a vile sorcerer and the most horrifying of images. And indeed we do. This story is by far the most disturbing we've read, filled with bloody basins and death by dismemberment.

Images of the Garden of Eden come to mind. A forest of trees with a particular tree in the middle that was forbidden, a tree of death, the tree of the knowledge of good and evil (Gen. 2:9). Did you hear the account of Genesis 2:16-17 when you read what the wizard said to the first pretty daughter?

> ...you may go everywhere and look at everything except into one room, which this little key opens, and there I forbid you to go on pain of death." He likewise gave her an egg and said, "Preserve the egg carefully for me, and carry it continually about with you, for a great misfortune would arise from the loss of it.

The wizard (the devil) being clever, but not original, reconstructs the Garden of Eden in his house of horror. He has his Eve in the pretty girls whom he catches, and with them in his house all seems perfect:

> Everything in the house was magnificent; he gave her whatsoever she could possibly desire, and said "My darling, you will certainly be happy with me, for you have everything your heart can wish for.

Eden's stage is set. There are good things all about and only one thing forbidden. His darling is even given to care for an egg, an obvious symbol of life. The mishandling of life, as was true in Eden, leads to death.

Of the three pretty daughters who we see brought to the house, only the third is not chopped into pieces for entering the room, and it's because the wizard doesn't know she entered it. Life and resurrection come with daughter number three. The wizard thinks she passed his test and therefore aims to make her his bride.

At this point in the story we begin to notice aspects of Jesus' words,

> And if a house is divided against itself, that house will not be able to stand. And if

> Satan has risen up against himself and is divided, he cannot stand, but is coming to an end. But no one can enter a strong man's house and plunder his goods, unless he first binds the strong man. Then indeed he may plunder his house (Mark 3:25-27).

The actions of the third daughter emphasize the binding of the strong man, whose would-be bride undoes the death he inflicts by confronting it in a way that removes his power, by converting his bloody basin full of hewn human beings into a baptismal font, where there is death to be sure, but from where life also emerges. She engages the gleaming axe and block of wood – the wizard's instrument of death – just like Christ faced the Roman cross, in a way that undid death's power and sting (1 Cor. 15:55-57).

Christ was resurrected on the *third* day. In like manner, the *third* daughter kept death's blood off life's egg and reassembled her sisters' bodies, concluding their resurrection with what amounts to the kiss of peace (Rom. 16:16; 1 Cor. 16:20; 2 Cor. 13:12; 1 Thess. 5:26; 1 Pet. 5:14).

This is a glorious scene that draws our attention to the truth Jesus spoke to Peter about the Church. "The gates of hell shall not prevail against it," Christ said. And "I will give you the keys of the kingdom of heaven, and whatever you bind on earth shall be bound in heaven, and whatever you loose on earth shall be loosed in heaven" (Matt. 16:18-19).

We're dealing with the downfall of our old evil foe, the binding of Satan by our Lord and His Church. We're dealing with keys. Not the keys the wicked wizard would give, keys to a sin-filled world – to a house in the middle of a dark forest – but the keys to heaven. Those are the keys the Bride of Christ holds, and, yes, they are the keys of life.

When the pretty girl, who stands in for the all those whom Jesus would have believe in him, cares for the egg (life) and is baptized, that is, goes into the wizard's forbidden room, she sees that which brings about death and, according to God's good will, also brings about life.

I wonder, is there any doubt why the wizard (Satan) would forbid the girl (us) from this one room, which is full of death? No. The room is a baptistry. Unlike the tree of knowledge of good and evil, which was forbidden because it would bring about man's death, the wizard's forbidden room is off limits because the evil one knows it will bring about his death.

The devil is undone when he returns to find no blood on the egg.

> "You have stood the test, you shall be my bride." He now had no longer any power over her, and was forced to do whatsoever she desired.

Indeed, for she is the Church, and she has been given the keys (by Christ). The wizard doesn't know it but his house is divided. With him bound, his affianced immediately begins to plunder his goods, and does so by his own manual labor. What inspiration! This pretty girl in effect says, "Act as if I'm yours, devil, and in the meantime I will prepare for the wedding... the true wedding with Christ."

In the preparation for the marriage feast of the Lamb, that is, in our earthly lives of faith, the devil goes about his plans thinking he's to have the Bride. But his power is undone. The Bride is not his, but another's. And she is not one to be underestimated.

The conclusion of the story depicts the fiery destruction of the devil and his demons – the wizard and his friends – who the bride invited to the marriage feast and lured into the house. "The wizard and all his crew had to burn." Or, in other words, "the devil who had deceived them was thrown into the lake of fire and sulfur where the beast and the false prophet were, and they will be tormented day and night forever and ever" (Rev. 20:10).

That's where the Brothers end their tale. But that's not the end of what Scripture says. After Revelation 20 comes 21. Had the Brothers' pen continued to reveal what happened to the bride in this story, would it not have been a fictionalized form of chapter 21?

> And I saw the holy city, new Jerusalem, coming down out of heaven from God, prepared as a bride adorned for her husband. And I heard a loud voice from the throne saying, "behold, the dwelling place of God is with man. He will dwell with them, and they will be his people, and God himself will be with them as their God. He will wipe away every tear from their eyes, and death shall be no more, neither shall

there be mourning, nor crying, nor pain anymore, for the former things have passed away (Rev. 21:2-4).

The Robber Bridegroom

THERE was once on a time a miller, who had a beautiful daughter, and as she was grown up, he wished that she was provided for, and well married. He thought, "If any good suitor comes and asks for her, I will give her to him."

Not long afterwards, a suitor came, who appeared to be very rich, and as the miller had no fault to find with him, he promised his daughter to him. The maiden, however, did not like him quite so much as a girl should like the man to whom she is engaged, and had no confidence in him. Whenever she saw, or thought of him, she felt a secret horror.

Once he said to her, "You are my betrothed, and yet you have never once paid me a visit."

The Robber Bridegroom

The maiden replied, "I know not where your house is."

Then said the bridegroom, "My house is out there in the dark forest."

She tried to excuse herself and said she could not find the way there. The bridegroom said, "Next Sunday you must come out there to me; I have already invited the guests, and I will scatter ashes in order that you may find thy way through the forest."

When Sunday came, and the maiden had to set out on her way, she became very uneasy, she herself knew not exactly why, and to mark her way she filled both her pockets full of peas and lentils. Ashes were scattered at the entrance of the forest, and these she followed, but at every step she threw a couple of peas on the ground. She walked almost the whole day until she reached the middle of the forest, where it was the darkest, and there stood a solitary house, which she did not like, for it looked so dark and dismal. She went inside it, but no one was within, and the most absolute stillness reigned.

Suddenly a voice cried,

"Turn back, turn back, young maiden dear,
'Tis a murderer's house you enter here."

The maiden looked up, and saw that the voice came from a bird, which was hanging in a cage on the wall. Again it cried,

*"Turn back, turn back, young maiden dear,
'Tis a murderer's house you enter here."*

Then the young maiden went on farther from one room to another, and walked through the whole house, but it was entirely empty and not one human being was to be found. At last she came to the cellar, and there sat an extremely aged woman, whose head shook constantly.

"Can you not tell me," said the maiden, "if my betrothed lives here?"

"Alas, poor child," replied the old woman, "from where have you come? You are in a murderer's den. You think you are a bride soon to be married, but you will keep your wedding with death. Look, I have been forced to put a great kettle on there, with water in it, and when they have you in their power, they will cut you to pieces without mercy, will cook you, and eat you, for they are eaters of human flesh. If I do

The Robber Bridegroom

not have compassion on you, and save you, you are lost."

After that the old woman led her behind a great hogshead where she could not be seen. "Be as still as a mouse," she said, "do not make a sound, or move, or all will be over with you. At night, when the robbers are asleep, we will escape; I have long waited for an opportunity."

Hardly was this done, than the godless crew came home. They dragged with them another young girl. They were drunk, and paid no heed to her screams and lamentations. They gave her wine to drink, three glasses full, one glass of white wine, one glass of red, and a glass of yellow, and with this her heart burst in two. After that they tore off her delicate raiment, laid her on a table, cut her beautiful body in pieces and scattered salt upon it. The poor bride behind the cask trembled and shook, for she saw right well what fate the robbers had destined for her.

One of them noticed a gold ring on the little finger of the murdered girl, and as it would not come off at once, he took an axe and cut the finger off, but it sprang up in the air, away over the cask and fell straight into the bride's bosom. The robber took a candle and wanted to look for it, but could not find it. Then another of them said, "Have you looked behind the great hogshead?"

But the old woman cried, "Come and get something to eat, and leave off looking till the morning, the finger won't run away from you."

Then the robbers said, "The old woman is right," and gave up their search, and sat down to eat, and the old woman poured a sleeping draught in their wine, so that they soon lay down in the cellar, and slept and snored.

When the bride heard that, she came out from behind the hogshead, and had to step over the sleepers, for they lay in rows on the ground, and great was her terror lest she should wake one of them. But God helped her, and she got safely over.

The old woman went up with her, opened the doors, and they hurried out of the murderers' den with all the speed in their power. The wind had blown away the scattered ashes, but the peas and lentils had sprouted and grown up, and showed them the way in the moonlight. They walked the whole night, until in the morning they arrived at the mill, and then the maiden told her father everything exactly as it had happened.

The Robber Bridegroom

When the day came when the wedding was to be celebrated, the bridegroom appeared, and the Miller had invited all his relations and friends. As they sat at table, each was bidden to relate something. The bride sat still, and said nothing.

Then the bridegroom said to the bride, "Come, my darling, do you know nothing? Relate something to us like the rest."

She replied, "Then I will relate a dream. I was walking alone through a wood, and at last I came to a house, in which no living soul was, but on the wall there was a bird in a cage which cried,

"Turn back, turn back, young maiden dear,
'Tis a murderer's house you enter here."

"And this it cried once more. My darling, I only dreamt this. Then I went through all the rooms, and they were all empty, and there was something so horrible about them! At last I went down into the cellar, and there sat a very very old woman, whose head shook; I asked her, 'Does my bridegroom live in this house? She answered, 'Alas poor child, you have got into a murderer's den, your bridegroom does live here, but he will hew you in pieces, and kill you, and then he will cook you, and eat you.' My darling, I only dreamt this. But the old woman hid me behind a great hogshead, and, scarcely was I hidden, when the robbers came home, dragging a maiden with them, to whom they gave three kinds of wine to drink, white, red, and yellow, with which her heart broke in two. My darling, I only dreamt this. After that they pulled off her pretty clothes, and hewed her fair body in pieces on a table, and sprinkled them with salt. My darling, I only dreamt this. And one of the robbers saw that there was still a ring on her little finger, and as it was hard to draw off, he took an axe and cut it off, but the finger sprang up in the air, and sprang behind the great hogshead, and fell in my bosom. And there is the finger with the ring!"

And with these words she drew it forth, and showed it to those present.

The robber, who had during this story become as pale as ashes, leapt up and wanted to escape, but the guests held him fast, and delivered him over to justice. Then he and his whole troop were executed for their infamous deeds.

The Robber Bridegroom

* * *

THIS story is not for the faint of heart. It's a terrible tale of horrific murder. A tale that, despite a brief encounter with a talking bird, could have actually occurred in a dark and depraved forest. Sadly, human beings are capable of such atrocities. I don't believe this story is intended to scare children, though such overt sin did scare my daughter when she read it. She even marked it in the table of contents so she would remember that it was too disturbing to read again. But this need not be the case.

Think about it this way: the story is dark and gory, but so is our world, right? Murder happens all the time in our world. You don't have to go to a bizarre episode in fairyland to find it. People lose life and limb for various reasons, including for their possessions, as did the beautiful girl who wore the ring. The storytellers don't mask the realities of living in a sin filled world, but instead confront it head on. They acknowledge the truth and are then able to overcome it. This story is one of encouragement. It delivers us into the trenches of our sinful condition and then provides the means by which we can escape. It shows us the benefits of keeping God's Law and the importance of serving our neighbor.

God established His good and holy Law to protect people from the horrors of sin, from devouring each other in our depravity. Consider the old woman, how she keeps the fifth commandment, "You shall not murder" (Ex. 20:13).

If she didn't do anything to save the betrothed bride, she would have been guilty of breaking this commandment, as guilty as the men carrying out the murderous act. Luther says it clearly in his explanation to the fifth commandment in his Small Catechism.

> "You shall not murder." What does this mean? We should fear and love God so that we do not hurt or harm our neighbor in his body, but help and support him in every physical need.

The commandments are not just prohibitions, but actually instructions in how we are to be of service to our neighbor. To keep the fifth commandment, the old woman had to help save the betrothed bride. Sadly, these two women were unable to save the beautiful girl as they escaped. They would have been overpowered and killed. But what did they do when they were finally free? The miller's daughter informed her father of what was going on, and a plan was hatched to bring justice to these murderous villains. In other words, the two escapees made sure the murderers would never harm another person, that is, they kept the fifth commandment.

We may not find ourselves in the same situation as the miller's daughter and the old woman (thank God!), but every day we have the opportunity to keep God's commandments as they did. As Christians we're saved by Christ's keeping the Law. We, therefore, strive to keep the commandments in like manner, not for ourselves, but for the welfare of our neighbor, just like the old woman served the miller's daughter, and like the miller's daughter served other girls who would've been victims of the Robber Bridegroom.

Old Hildebrand

ONCE upon a time lived a peasant and his wife, and the parson of the village had a fancy for the wife, and had wished for a long while to spend a whole day happily with her. The peasant woman, too, was quite willing. One day, therefore, he said to the woman, "Listen, my dear friend, I have now thought of a way by which we can for once spend a whole day happily together. I'll tell you what; on Wednesday, you must take to your bed, and tell your husband you are ill, and if you only complain and act being ill properly, and go on doing so until Sunday when I have to preach, I will then say in my sermon that whosoever has at home a sick child, a sick husband, a sick wife, a sick father, a sick mother, a sick brother or

Old Hildebrand

whosoever else it may be, and makes a pilgrimage to the Göckerli hill in Italy, where you can get a peck of laurel leaves for a kreuzer, the sick child, the sick husband, the sick wife, the sick father, or sick mother, the sick sister, or whosoever else it may be, will be restored to health immediately."

"I will manage it," said the woman promptly.

Now therefore on the Wednesday, the peasant woman took to her bed, and complained and lamented as agreed on, and her husband did everything for her that he could think of, but nothing did her any good, and when Sunday came the woman said, "I feel as ill as if I were going to die at once, but there is one thing I should like to do before my end I should like to hear the parson's sermon that he is going to preach today."

On that the peasant said, "Ah, my child, do not do it—you might make yourself worse if you were to get up. Look, I will go to the sermon, and will attend to it very carefully, and will tell you everything the parson says."

"Well," said the woman, "go, then, and pay great attention, and repeat to me all that you hear."

So the peasant went to the sermon, and the parson began to preach and said, if anyone had at home a sick child, a sick husband, a sick wife, a sick father a sick mother, a sick sister, brother or anyone else, and would make a pilgrimage to the Göckerli hill in Italy, where a peck of laurel leaves costs a kreuzer, the sick child, sick husband, sick wife, sick father, sick mother, sick sister, brother, or whosoever else it might be, would be restored to health instantly, and whosoever wished to undertake the journey was to go to him after the service was over, and he would give him the sack for the laurel leaves and the kreuzer.

Then no one was more rejoiced than the peasant, and after the service was over, he went at once to the parson, who gave him the bag for the laurel leaves and the kreuzer. After that he went home, and even at the house door he cried, "Hurrah! dear wife, it is now almost the same thing as if you were well! The parson has preached today that whosoever had at home a sick child, a sick husband, a sick wife, a sick father, a sick mother, a sick sister, brother or whoever it might be, and would make a pilgrimage to the Göckerli hill in Italy, where a peck of laurel leaves costs a kreuzer, the sick

Old Hildebrand

child, sick husband, sick wife, sick father, sick mother, sick sister, brother, or whosoever else it was, would be cured immediately, and now I have already got the bag and the kreuzer from the parson, and will at once begin my journey so that you may get well the faster," and after that he went away. He was, however, hardly gone before the woman got up, and the parson was there directly.

But now we will leave these two for a while, and follow the peasant, who walked on quickly without stopping, in order to get the sooner to the Göckerli hill, and on his way he met his gossip. His gossip was an egg merchant, and was just coming from the market, where he had sold his eggs. "May you be blessed," said the gossip, "where are you off to so fast?"

"To all eternity, my friend," said the peasant, "my wife is ill, and I have been today to hear the parson's sermon, and he preached that if anyone had in his house a sick child, a sick husband, a sick wife, a sick father, a sick mother, a sick sister, brother or anyone else, and made a pilgrimage to the Göckerli hill in Italy, where a peck of laurel leaves costs a kreuzer, the sick child, the sick husband, the sick wife, the sick father, the sick mother, the sick sister, brother or whosoever else it was, would be cured immediately, and so I have got the bag for the laurel leaves and the kreuzer from the parson, and now I am beginning my pilgrimage."

"But listen, gossip," said the egg merchant to the peasant, "are you, then, stupid enough to believe such a thing as that? Don't you know what it means? The parson wants to spend a whole day alone with your wife in peace, so he has given you this job to do to get you out of the way."

"My word!" said the peasant. "How I'd like to know if that's true!"

"Come, then," said the gossip, "I'll tell you what to do. Get into my egg basket and I will carry you home, and then you will see for yourself." So that was settled, and the gossip put the peasant into his egg basket and carried him home.

When they got to the house, hurrah! but all was going merry there! The woman had already had nearly everything killed that was in the farmyard, and had made pancakes, and the parson was there, and had brought his fiddle with him. The gossip knocked at the door, and woman asked who was there.

Old Hildebrand

"It is I, gossip," said the egg merchant, "give me shelter this night; I have not sold my eggs at the market, so now I have to carry them home again, and they are so heavy that I shall never be able to do it, for it is dark already."

"Indeed, my friend," said the woman, "you come at a very inconvenient time for me, but as you are here it can't be helped, come in, and take a seat there on the bench by the stove." Then she placed the gossip and the basket which he carried on his back on the bench by the stove.

The parson, however, and the woman, were as merry as possible. At length the parson said, "Listen, my dear friend, you can sing beautifully; sing something to me."

"Oh," said the woman, "I cannot sing now, in my young days indeed I could sing well enough, but that's all over now."

"Come," said the parson once more, "do sing some little song."

On that the woman began and sang,

*"I've sent my husband away from me
To the Göckerli hill in Italy."*

Thereupon the parson sang,

> *"I wish 'twas a year before he came back,*
> *I'd never ask him for the laurel leaf sack.*
> > *Hallelujah."*

Then the gossip who was in the background began to sing (but I ought to tell you the peasant was called Hildebrand), so the gossip sang,

> *"What art thou doing, my Hildebrand dear, There on the bench by the stove so near?*
> > *Hallelujah."*

And then the peasant sang from his basket,

> *"All singing I ever shall hate from this day,*
> *And here in this basket no longer I'll stay.*
> > *Hallelujah."*

And he got out of the basket, and cudgeled the parson out of the house.

* * *

HERE we're able to see God's Word in the words of men quite easily. Not only do we have before us another story that extends from the Ten Commandments, we have a story that deals directly with the pastoral office. Thank heavens, it is clearly established as a work of fiction, opening with the ever familiar, "Once upon a time." Otherwise, the reality of the parson's actions would be unbearable.

Who are we kidding?

Clergymen are sinners like everyone else. This story could very well have been inspired by an actual event. Pastors, though servants of God, are not immune to trespassing against God and neighbor in such an abhorrent manner. We know it happens. This tale reveals the consequences that come with abusing one's vocation, in particular, that of pastor.

What commandment is most explicitly at play in this tale? The tenth. Exodus 20:17.

> "You shall not covet your neighbor's wife, or his manservant or maidservant, his ox or donkey, or anything that belongs to your neighbor."

> And what does this mean? "We should fear and love God so that we do not entice or force away our neighbor's wife, workers, or

> animals, or turn them against him, but urge them to stay and do their duty."²²

The parson coveted the peasant's wife "and had wished for a long while to spend a whole day happily with her." His coveting was apparently known to the wife for we're told that she "too, was quite willing." He was certainly not urging her to stay and do her duty to her husband. This covetous desire took hold of him and manifested into outward sin, not just against the peasant and his wife, but against the entire congregation of saints under his care. It would seem that we have before us an allusion to James 1:14-15, "But each person is tempted when he is lured and enticed by his own desire. Then desire when it has conceived gives birth to sin, and sin when it is fully grown brings forth death."

The parson acted on his desire, which gave birth to sin. That sin, fully grown, brought forth death, the death of old Hildebrand, who sang, "I ever shall hate from this day." The peasant trusted the church. He trusted the parson. And that trust was violated, permanently planting

---

[22] Martin Luther, *Luther's Small Catechism* (St. Louis: Concordia Publishing House, 2008), 13-14.

hatred in his heart. Not only was he sinned against, but from that day he became a sinner in a particular way. From that day on he would forever break the fifth commandment, having murder in his heart. The parson created unrepentant sin in the man he wronged. He brought forth death.

Hildebrand says his hatred is directed toward singing. You may think that's not a big deal. It is. Consider the following Bible passages: Psalm 13:6; 33:3; 40:3; 96:1; 105:2; and 1 Chronicles 16:23 (to name a few). They reveal the depth of his hatred. Hildebrand hates the way God's people respond to His love, singing. An argument could be made that by declaring his hatred of all song old Hildebrand announced that he hated all worship of the Lord.

The abuse of the pastoral office has grave consequences.

One wonders about the rest of the story. How might it have continued? What ungodly chaos might have ensued among the church as a result of this trespass? The parson's sinful plot to spend time with Hildebrand's wife did, after all, involve the fabrication of false doctrine, which was preached to the Church on

Sunday. He was willing to lead Christ's people away from true teaching to suit his own desires. Are not all false teachings hatched from the false prophet's own sinful desires? Indeed, they are. He broke trust with the entire congregation. How many would never get over such a violation of office? Would others hate singing to the Lord from that day forward?

Unfortunately, this exact sin happens in real life. When it occurs, it causes real pain. Pain that blots forgiveness from man's heart and brings about death. It is for this reason that pastors are to take their office seriously, not as an opportunity for self-gain, but as a humble service to neighbor. James 3:1 comes to mind. "Not many of you should become teachers, my brothers, for you know that we who teach will be judged with greater strictness."

Pastors are to take their office seriously, especially because they've been called to guide people in the truth, which puts them in a position to lead people astray if they're not faithful to Scripture. Of course, this isn't to say others shouldn't take their vocations seriously as well. This tale draws from God's Word, teaching us to serve our neighbor faithfully.

Old Hildebrand

Just look at the behavior of old Hildebrand. He lovingly served his wife. Concerned for her health, he insisted that she stay home from church so she could rest.

> You might make yourself worse if you were to get up. Look I will go to the sermon, and will attend to it very carefully, and will tell you everything the parson says.

Do you see the image of a husband hanging on every word of the sermon, taking notes to bring home to his wife? What loving service! And when this husband hears how his wife can get better, he immediately sets out to do what needs to be done. He was living out his vocation of husband faithfully.

We see another Christian living out his vocation faithfully as well. This tale involves a gossip, the husband's gossip. Do you remember what we learned about gossips when we considered *The Little Peasant*? If not you'll have to take my word that the husband meets his godfather, the man who was called to provide spiritual guidance to Hildebrand when he was baptized. He's on his pilgrimage when he meets "his gossip." Not *a* gossip, *his* gossip.

His gossip, after learning what Hildebrand is up to, asks him if he was so stupid as to believe the false teaching of the parson, and then helps him see the truth. The gossip knew Scripture. He knew God's Word said nothing about pilgrimages to Göckerli hill in Italy. What a blessed layman.

Dear reader, be like the gossip. Be wise in the Word and know the truth, so that when false teachers try to pull the wool over your eyes, you'll be able to see through sinful words and guide others back to the truth.

If we can speculate for a moment and go where the story does not, I'd like to suggest, based on what we've seen in this tale, that though the desire of the parson gave birth to sin, the death that was brought forth was conquered by the gossip. He was Hildebrand's godfather in Christ, after all. And we see that he carried out his calling faithfully. After Hildebrand cudgeled the parson out of the house, I'd like to think that the gossip began guiding his godchild away from hatred and toward forgiveness, thereby saving him from eternal death.

What do you think? If the story continued, would we see that happen?

The Singing Bone

IN a certain country there was once great lamentation over a wild boar that laid waste the farmer's fields, killed the cattle, and ripped up people's bodies with his tusks. The King promised a large reward to anyone who would free the land from this plague; but the beast was so big and strong that no one dared to go near the forest in which it lived.

At last the King gave notice that whosoever should capture or kill the wild boar should have his only daughter to wife.

Now there lived in the country two brothers, sons of a poor man, who declared themselves willing to undertake the hazardous enterprise; the elder, who was crafty and shrewd, out of pride; the younger, who was innocent and simple, from a kind heart.

The King said, "In order that you may be the more sure of finding the beast, you must go into the forest from opposite sides." So the elder went in on the west side, and the younger on the east.

When the younger had gone a short way, a little man stepped up to him. He held in his hand a black spear and said, "I give you this spear because your heart is pure and good; with this you can boldly attack the wild boar, and it will do you no harm."

He thanked the little man, shouldered the spear, and went on fearlessly. Before long he saw the beast, which rushed at him; but he held the spear towards it, and in its blind fury it ran so swiftly against it that its heart was cloven in two. Then he took the monster on his back and went homewards with it to the King.

As he came out at the other side of the wood, there stood at the entrance a house where people were making merry with wine and dancing. His elder brother had gone in here, and, thinking that after all the boar would not run away from him, was going to drink until he felt brave. But when he saw his young

The Singing Bone

brother coming out of the wood laden with his booty, his envious, evil heart gave him no peace. He called out to him, "Come in, dear brother, rest and refresh yourself with a cup of wine."

The youth, who suspected no evil, went in and told him about the good little man who had given him the spear with which he had slain the boar.

The elder brother kept him there until the evening, and then they went away together, and when in the darkness they came to a bridge over a brook, the elder brother let the other go first; and when he was halfway across he gave him such a blow from behind that he fell down dead.

He buried him beneath the bridge, took the boar, and carried it to the King, pretending that he had killed it; whereupon he obtained the King's daughter in marriage. And when his younger brother did not come back he said, "The boar must have killed him," and every one believed it.

But as nothing remains hidden from God, so this black deed also was to come to light.

Years afterwards a shepherd was driving his herd across the bridge, and saw lying in the sand beneath, a snow white little bone. He thought that it would make a good mouthpiece, so he clambered down, picked it up, and cut out of it a mouthpiece for his horn. But when he blew through it for the first time, to his great astonishment, the bone began of its own accord to sing:

> *"Ah, friend, you blow upon my bone!*
> *Long have I laid beside the water;*
> *My brother slew me for the boar,*
> *And took for his wife the King's young daughter."*

"What a wonderful horn!" said the shepherd; "it sings by itself; I must take it to my lord the King." And when he came with it to the King the horn again began to sing its little song. The King understood it all, and caused the ground below the bridge to be dug up, and then the whole skeleton of the murdered man came to light. The wicked brother could not deny the deed, and was sewn up in a sack and drowned. But the bones of the murdered man were laid to rest in a beautiful tomb in the churchyard.

* * *

The Singing Bone

THE tale of two brothers. A story almost as old as boy-meets-girl. After all, first there was Adam and Eve, then there was Cain and Abel. That's what we have before us in here. Like with Cain, sin was crouching at the oldest brother's door. If only he would've ruled over it (Gen. 4:7).

When the younger of the two brothers does well in the forest, the elder, who is described as "crafty and shrewd, out of pride," sees his success and murders him. This was exactly how things happened in Genesis. Cain grew "very angry, and his face fell" (Gen. 4:5). Or as we just read, "his envious, evil heart gave him no peace."

So what did Cain do?

> Cain spoke to Abel his brother. And when they were in the field, Cain rose up against his brother Abel and killed him (Gen. 4:8).

What did the eldest brother in our story do?

> He called out to him... and then they went away together, and when in the darkness... [he] gave him such a blow from behind that he fell down dead.

O, the treachery! Where's the justice? The older brother in our tale gets the girl when the younger should have. And just like the vile deed committed against Joseph by his brothers (Gen. 37:29-34) – another account of brother(s) sinning against brother – he deceives everyone, declaring that "the boar must have killed" his younger brother. Who wouldn't believe that the fierce animal devoured him (Gen. 37:33)?

But never fear, my friends, justice is served. Both in real life and in the Grimm's fairyland extension of it. As they said, "But as nothing remains hidden from God, so this black deed also was to come to light."

God is omniscient (all-knowing), omnipotent (almighty), and omnipresent (present everywhere). We cannot keep our sins from Him. We may try our best to conceal our evil deeds, we can carry them out under the shroud of darkness, it doesn't matter, "nothing remains hidden from God." He will uncover the deeps out of darkness and bring deep darkness to light (Job 12:22). There are plenty of Scripture passages that deal with justice and God bringing vengeance on the evil doer, but perhaps considering Psalm 37:28 will be sufficient for our purposes.

> For the LORD loves the just and will not forsake his faithful ones. Wrongdoers will be completely destroyed; the offspring of the wicked will perish.

God did not forsake Abel. Cain killed his younger brother whose blood cried out to God from the ground (Gen. 4:11). God heard this cry and answered it by dealing directly with Cain, but also, years later, by sending His Son, Jesus, to take on flesh and be killed like Abel. Jesus is the mediator of a new covenant whose sprinkled blood speaks a better word than Abel's blood (Heb. 12:24). Christ came to defeat the grave once and for all, so that the ground that opened its mouth and received the blood of the faithful would be defanged (Gen. 4:11; Is. 25:8; 1 Cor. 15:54-58) and swallowed up forever.

This reality is conveyed in our tale when a shepherd brings the truth to light. A *shepherd?* Go figure (see John 10:11)! He reveals the dark past by uncovering the younger brother's bone, which sings out just like Abel's blood.

What else did you notice? Tell me you took note of the story's conclusion. What happened to the two brothers? The wicked brother is drowned as a part of the baptismal truth that is being presented. In baptism the sinner is drowned while the innocent Christian man is given life.

Wait a minute. But the younger brother isn't alive at the end. He's dead.

Is he? Death was defeated by Jesus. For the Christian, death is the consummation of baptism. What was started at the font comes to completion in the churchyard (cemetery) as the believer's soul – "innocent and simple, from a kind heart" – is brought into the presence of Christ at the throne of God. The body of the younger brother, who spent a long time beside the water (we spend the length of our days *beside the water* of baptism) is laid to rest in a beautiful tomb in the churchyard. That is, he's given the Christian rest that comes in the Gospel of Christ Jesus. He is given life, even if you and I cannot see it on this side of our Lord's second coming.

Maid Maleen

THERE was once a King who had a son who asked in marriage the daughter of a mighty King; she was called Maid Maleen, and was very beautiful. As her father wished to give her to another, the prince was rejected; but as they both loved each other with all their hearts, they would not give each other up, and Maid Maleen said to her father, "I can and will take no other for my husband."

Then the King flew into a passion, and ordered a dark tower to be built, into which no ray of sunlight or moonlight should enter. When it was finished, he said, "Therein shall you be imprisoned for seven years, and then I will come and see if your perverse spirit is broken."

Meat and drink for the seven years were carried into the tower, and then she and her waiting-woman were led into it and walled up, and thus cut off from the sky and from the earth. There they sat in the darkness, and knew not when day or night began.

The King's son often went around and around the tower, and called their names, but no sound from without pierced through the thick walls.

What else could they do but lament and complain?

Meanwhile the time passed, and by the diminution of the food and drink they knew that the seven years were coming to an end. They thought the moment of their deliverance was come; but no stroke of the hammer was heard, no stone fell out of the wall, and it seemed to Maid Maleen that her father had forgotten her. As they only had food for a short time longer, and saw a miserable death awaiting them, Maid Maleen said, "We must try our last chance, and see if we can break through the wall."

She took the breadknife, and picked and bored at the mortar of a stone, and when she was tired, the waiting-maid took her turn. With

Maid Maleen

great labor they succeeded in getting out one stone, and then a second, and a third, and when three days were over the first ray of light fell on their darkness, and at last the opening was so large that they could look out.

The sky was blue, and a fresh breeze played on their faces; but how melancholy everything looked all around! Her father's castle lay in ruins, the town and the villages were, so far as could be seen, destroyed by fire, the fields far and wide laid to waste, and no human being was visible.

When the opening in the wall was large enough for them to slip through, the waiting-maid sprang down first, and then Maid Maleen followed. But where were they to go? The enemy had ravaged the whole kingdom, driven away the King, and slain all the inhabitants.

They wandered forth to seek another country, but nowhere did they find a shelter, or a human being to give them a mouthful of bread, and their need was so great that they were forced to appease their hunger with nettles. When, after long journeying, they came into another country, they tried to get work everywhere; but wherever they knocked they were turned away, and no one would have pity on them.

At last they arrived in a large city and went to the royal palace. There also they were ordered to go away, but at last the cook said that they might stay in the kitchen and be scullions.

The son of the King in whose kingdom they were, was, however, the very man who had been betrothed to Maid Maleen. His father had chosen another bride for him, whose face was as ugly as her heart was wicked. The wedding was fixed, and the maiden had already arrived; but because of her great ugliness, however, she shut herself in her room, and allowed no one to see her, and Maid Maleen had to take her her meals from the kitchen.

When the day came for the bride and the bridegroom to go to church, she was ashamed of her ugliness, and afraid that if she showed herself in the streets, she would be mocked and laughed at by the people. Then said she to Maid Maleen, "A great piece of luck has befallen you. I have sprained my foot, and cannot well walk through the streets; you shall put on my wedding clothes and take my place; a greater honor than that you cannot have!"

Maid Maleen, however, refused it, and said, "I wish for no honor which is not suitable for me."

It was in vain, too, that the bride offered her gold. At last she said angrily, "If you do not obey me, it shall cost you your life. I have but to speak the word, and your head will lie at your feet."

Then she was forced to obey, and put on the bride's magnificent clothes and all her jewels. When she entered the royal hall, everyone was amazed at her great beauty, and the King said to his son, "This is the bride whom I have chosen for you, and whom you must lead to church."

The bridegroom was astonished, and thought, "She is like my Maid Maleen, and I should believe that it was she herself, but she has long been shut up in the tower, or dead." He took her by the hand and led her to church.

On the way was a nettle plant, and she said,

"Oh, nettle plant,
Little nettle plant,
What do you here alone?
I have known the time
When I ate you unboiled,

When I ate you unroasted."

"What are you saying?" asked the King's son.

"Nothing," she replied, "I was only thinking of Maid Maleen."

He was surprised that she knew about her, but kept silence.

When they came to the foot plank into the churchyard, she said,

*"Foot bridge, do not break,
I am not the true bride."*

"What are you saying there?" asked the King's son.

"Nothing," she replied, "I was only thinking of Maid Maleen."

"Do you know Maid Maleen?"

"No," she answered, "how should I know her; I have only heard of her." When they came to the church door, she said once more,

*"Church door, break not,
I am not the true bride."*

"What are you saying there?" he asked.

Maid Maleen

"Ah," she answered, "I was only thinking of Maid Maleen."

Then he took out a precious chain, put it around her neck, and fastened the clasp. After that they entered the church, and the priest joined their hands together before the altar, and married them. He led her home, but she did not speak a single word the whole way.

When they got back to the royal palace, she hurried into the bride's chamber, put off the magnificent clothes and the jewels, dressed herself in her gray gown, and kept nothing but the jewel on her neck, which she had received from the bridegroom.

When the night came, and the bride was to be led into the prince's apartment, she let her veil fall over her face, that he might not observe the deception.

As soon as everyone had gone away, he said to her, "What did you say to the nettle plant which was growing by the wayside?"

"To which nettle plant?" she asked; "I don't talk to nettle plants."

"If you did not do it, then you are not the true bride," he said.

So she thought to herself, and said,

"I must go out unto my maid,
Who keeps my thoughts for me."

She went out and sought Maid Maleen. "Girl, what have you been saying to the nettle?"
"I said nothing but,

Oh, nettle-plant,
Little nettle plant,
What do you here alone?
I have known the time
When I ate you unboiled,
When I ate you unroasted."

The bride ran back into the chamber, and said, "I know now what I said to the nettle," and she repeated the words which she had just heard.

"But what did you say to the foot bridge when we went over it?" asked the King's son.

"To the foot bridge?" she answered. "I don't talk to foot bridges."

"Then you are not the true bride."

She again said,

"I must go out unto my maid,
Who keeps my thoughts for me,"

And ran out and found Maid Maleen, "Girl, what did you say to the foot bridge?"

"I said nothing but,

*"Footbridge, do not break,
I am not the true bride."*

"That costs you your life!" cried the bride, but she hurried into the room, and said, "I know now what I said to the foot bridge," and she repeated the words.

"But what did you say to the church door?"

"To the church door?" she replied; "I don't talk to church doors."

"Then you are not the true bride."

She went out and found Maid Maleen, and said, "Girl, what did you say to the church door?"

"I said nothing but,

*"Church door, break not,
I am not the true bride."*

"That will break your neck for you!" cried the bride, and flew into a terrible passion, but she hastened back into the room, and said, "I know now what I said to the church door," and she repeated the words.

"But where do you have the jewel which I gave you at the church door?"

"What jewel?" she answered; "you did not give me any jewel."

"I myself put it around your neck, and I myself fastened it; if you do not know that, you are not the true bride." He drew the veil from her face, and when he saw her immeasurable ugliness, he sprang back terrified, and said, "How come you are here? Who are you?"

"I am your betrothed bride, but because I feared lest the people should mock me when they saw me out of doors, I commanded the scullery maid to dress herself in my clothes, and to go to church instead of me."

"Where is the girl?" he said; "I want to see her, go and bring her here."

She went out and told the servants that the scullery maid was an impostor, and that they must take her out into the courtyard and strike off her head.

The servants laid hold of Maid Maleen and wanted to drag her out, but she screamed so loudly for help, that the King's son heard her voice, hurried out of his chamber and ordered them to set the maiden free instantly.

Lights were brought, and then he saw on her neck the gold chain which he had given her at the church door.

"You are the true bride," he said, "who went with me to the church; come with me now to my room." When they were both alone, he said, "On the way to church you did name Maid Maleen, who was my betrothed bride; if I could believe it possible, I should think she was standing before me for you are like her in every respect."

She answered, "I am Maid Maleen, who for your sake was imprisoned seven years in the darkness, who suffered hunger and thirst, and has lived so long in want and poverty. Today, however, the sun is shining on me once more. I was married to you in the church, and I am your lawful wife."

Then they kissed each other, and were happy all the days of their lives. The false bride was rewarded for what she had done by having her head cut off.

The tower in which Maid Maleen had been imprisoned remained standing for a long time, and when the children passed by it they sang,

Finding the Truth in Story

"Kling, klang, gloria.
Who sits within this tower?
A King's daughter, she sits within,
A sight of her I cannot win,
The wall it will not break,
The stone cannot be pierced.
Little Hans, with your coat so gay,
Follow me, follow me, fast as you may."

* * *

THERE is a push these days to retell fairytales so that the damsel in distress saves not only herself but also the not-so-valiant, usually bumbling, incompetent oaf of a prince. These efforts to empower young girls not to need a knight in shining armor to save them, while commendable from the perspective that girls are strong creatures in their own right, are misplaced and work to build animosity between man and woman – the lover and the beloved – and ultimately the Savior and the saved. Besides, there is no need to alter a story to fit the feminist agenda when fairy tales already exist with strong female protagonists – locked up in dark towers by cruel kings – who rescue themselves and go on to save the princes. *Maid Maleen* is one such story.

Of course, it's also more than that. The immediate actions of Maid Maleen reflect the bigger–unrecognized by the world–actions of God to bring His people to Himself. It's a story of Christ and His bride. While the Grimm brothers' tale focuses on the actions of Maleen, it's still a tale of the love our Lord has for His faithful bride, the Church. Maleen's willingness to suffer in the tower for seven years is akin to the Christian's willingness to suffer all things for Christ. She says as much toward the end of the story when she, using language reminiscent of the beatitudes (Matt. 5:3, 6), tells the prince who she is.

> I am Maid Maleen, who *for your sake* was imprisoned seven years in the darkness, who suffered hunger and thirst, and has lived so long in want and poverty. (emphasis mine)

The Prince and his bride will be wed. Christ and His Church are to be united at the marriage feast of the lamb (Rev. 19:7-8). There is nothing that can keep this from happening. The words of the fairy tale before us would appear to extend from the following Word of God found in Romans 8:35-39,

> Who shall separate us from the love of Christ? Shall tribulation, or distress, or persecution, or famine, or nakedness, or danger, or sword? As it is written,
>
>> "For your sake we are being killed all the day long;
>> we are regarded as sheep to be slaughtered."
>
> No, in all these things we are more than conquerors through him who loved us. For I am sure that neither death nor life, nor angels nor rulers, nor things present nor things to come, nor powers, nor height nor depth, nor anything else in all creation, will be able to separate us from the love of God in Christ Jesus our Lord.

Who shall separate Maid Maleen from the love of the prince? Shall "the King who flew into a passion, and ordered a dark tower to be built, into which no ray of sunlight or moonlight should enter"? How about the ruin of the castle, the burning of the towns and villages of her kingdom, and the fields laid to waste?

No, in all these things she is more than a conqueror through God who loved her. For we can be sure that neither the enemy that ravaged the whole kingdom, that drove away the king, and killed all the inhabitants, nor the hunger that forced her to eat the stinging nettle plant, nor being turned away from everyone from whom she sought help, nor being a maid to a betrothed bride who threatens to kill her, nor anything else in all creation will be able to separate her from the love of God in the prince whom she will, before the end of the story, wed.

That's the gist of the entire story. But, before we move on to the next tale, let's consider some of the details. For instance, the darkness of Maleen's tower. Apart from Christ we're in darkness, utter and complete darkness. If we were cut off from our Lord, one might use the words of this story to rightly ask, "What else could they do but lament and complain?"

We learn that the prince goes around and around the tower, calling the names of Maleen and her waiting woman. Those who live in isolation from God, are separated from his

Word, from His calling their names. He is calling their names, but they do not hear Him. To be cut off from God is to be deaf to His calling our names (Is. 43:1), to not hear the preaching of His Word, which works faith in our hearts (Rom. 10:14). We might as well be in a tower, cut off from all "sunlight or moonlight" (John 1:4-5, 9), unable to hear (Matt. 13:9, 43; Mark 4:9, 23; Luke 8:8, 35; Rev. 2:7, 11, 3:6).

Maleen was imprisoned for seven years, which is a familiar length of time to the Christian. Jacob worked seven years to earn Rachel's hand in marriage (Genesis 29:18). The reader who remembers this Old Testament story has an advantage in understanding where the Grimm brothers are going with their tale. It foreshadows the plot that develops once Maleen escapes the tower, a three-day effort to remove a stone where then "the first ray of light fell on their darkness." Yes, you would do well to see an allusion to Jesus rising from the tomb on the third day by rolling back the stone that sealed him in, that blocked all sunlight. This is our story's resurrection moment. Maleen, who the prince thinks long dead, is alive!

But how is it that Jacob and Rachel foreshadow the prince and Maleen? For starters, both couples must wait seven years before they're united in marriage. Furthermore, it's only after seven years that another woman enters the picture. In Genesis it's Leah with her weak eyes (Gen. 29:17) in contrast to Rachel's beauty. In *Maid Maleen* it's a bride his father chose for him "whose face was as ugly as her wicked heart."

Jacob is deceived by Laban (his soon to be father-in-law) when in the evening, under the cover of darkness, he chooses to send Leah to be united with Jacob. It isn't until morning, in the light, that Jacob discovers he's been deceived (Gen. 29:21-25). Similarly, the prince is expecting to marry one woman but is deceived and ends up marrying another. The difference is that the deception that the prince suffers in our story works to his benefit. He is finally married to his betrothed–true bride– from seven years ago.

Darkness is also involved in both deceptions to conceal the brides' true identities. Jacob discovers the deception in the morning light (after he's already married to Leah) whereas the prince brings in lights before it's too late, discovering the gold chain he placed around Maleen's neck at the church.

We see in both accounts (Biblical and fictional) that in a fallen world God is able to work through sin. He doesn't approve of sin, but he does work through it to carry out His will. The fairyland deception leads to the prince (Jesus) and His bride (the Church) being wed. What the ugly bride meant for evil (self-good), God used for true good (Gen. 50:20). This can even be extended to include the cruelty of Maleen's father. His sinful imprisonment of his daughter was, after all, repurposed to bring the prince and Maleen together in the end.

Finally, consider this last thought. The prince's true bride is the lawful wife he married in the church – Maid Maleen who stood in for the ugly bride. The ugly deceitful bride-to-be was the actual imposter as she has to continually go back to the bride to learn what she said during the wedding. The same goes for Christ's bride, the Christian Church. I propose that the false bride in our story represents the unbelieving Jews who, though in the flesh they come from God's chosen people, they do not have faith in Christ, and therefore are not truly His bride. Jesus is described as the head of the body, His church (Col. 1:18), and like the ugly would-be bride adherents to the Jewish religion have lost their head. "The false bride was rewarded for what she had done by having her head cut off."

God's chosen people have always been those who trusted in His promise of salvation. Above I mentioned that this story extends from God's Word in Romans 8:35-39. It does, and it continues with verses 1-8 that follow in chapter nine:

> I am speaking the truth in Christ—I am not lying; my conscience bears me witness in the Holy Spirit—that I have great sorrow and unceasing anguish in my heart. For I could wish that I myself were accursed and *cut off from Christ* for the sake of my brothers, my kinsmen according to the flesh. They are Israelites, and to them belong the adoption, the glory, the covenants, the giving of the law, the worship, and the promises. To them belong the patriarchs, and from their race, according to the flesh, is the Christ, who is God over all, blessed forever. Amen.

> But it is not as though the word of God has failed. For not all who are descended from Israel belong to Israel, and not all are children of Abraham because they are his offspring, but 'Through Isaac shall your offspring be named.' This means that *it is not the children of the flesh who are the children of God, but the children of the promise are counted as offspring.* (emphasis mine)

It's not the false bride who is the true bride, though she was chosen by the prince's father. Maleen is the true and lawful bride because of the wedding promise that binds her in faith to her bridegroom. What a wonderful story of hope for anyone who believes in Christ. We are Maleen! When we have moments in life where we doubt the love of God, where we say to ourselves, "I am not the true bride," we speak nonsense. The Prince has placed his precious chain around the necks of those whom he loves and he fastened the clasp. Those who believe are part of the Church and the Christian Church is his true bride with whom He has joined hands. We are truly, lawfully His. Nothing can separate us from the love of God in Christ Jesus our Lord.

The Skillful Huntsman

THERE was once a young fellow who had learned the trade of locksmith, and told his father he would now go out into the world and seek his fortune.

"Very well," said the father, "I am quite content with that," and gave him some money for his journey.

So he travelled about and looked for work. After a time he resolved not to follow the trade of locksmith any more, for he no longer liked it, but he took a fancy for hunting. Then there met him in his rambles a huntsman dressed in green, who asked from where he came and where he was going? The youth said he was a locksmith's apprentice, but that the trade no longer pleased him, and he had a liking for huntsmanship, would he teach it to him?

"Oh, yes," said the huntsman, "if you will go with me."

Then the young fellow went with him, bound himself to him for some years, and learned the art of hunting.

After this he wished to try his luck elsewhere, and the huntsman gave him nothing in the way of payment but an air gun, which had, however, this property, that it hit its mark without fail whenever he shot with it.

Then he set out and found himself in a very large forest, which he could not get to the end of in one day. When evening came he seated himself in a high tree in order to escape from the wild beasts. Towards midnight, it seemed to him as if a tiny little light glimmered in the distance. Then he looked down through the branches towards it, and kept well in his mind where it was. But in the first place he took off his hat and threw it down in the direction of the light, so that he might go to the hat as a mark when he had descended.

Then he got down and went to his hat, put it on again and went straight forwards. The farther he went, the larger the light grew, and when he got close to it he saw that it was an enormous fire, and that three giants were sitting by it, who had an ox on the spit, and were roasting it. Presently one of them said, "I must just taste if the meat will soon be fit to eat," and pulled a piece off, and was about to put it in his mouth when the huntsman shot it out of his hand. "Well, really," said the giant, "if the wind has not blown the bit out of my hand!" and helped himself to another.

But when he was just about to bite into it, the huntsman again shot it away from him. On this the giant gave the one who was sitting next him a box on the ear, and cried angrily, "Why are you snatching my piece away from me?"

"I have not snatched it away," said the other, "a sharpshooter must have shot it away from you."

The giant took another piece, but could not, however, keep it in his hand, for the huntsman shot it out. Then the giant said, "That must be a good shot to shoot the bit out of one's very mouth, such an one would be useful to us." And he cried aloud, "Come here, you sharpshooter, seat yourself at the fire beside us and eat your fill, we will not hurt you; but if you will not come, and we have to bring you by force, you are a lost man!"

On this the youth went up to them and told them he was a skilled huntsman, and that whatever he aimed at with his gun, he was certain to hit. Then they said if he would go with them he should be well treated, and they told him that outside the forest there was a great lake, behind which stood a tower, and in the tower was imprisoned a lovely princess, whom they wished very much to carry off.

"Yes," he said, "I will soon get her for you."

Then they added, "But there is still something else, there is a tiny little dog, which begins to bark directly any one goes near, and as soon as it barks everyone in the royal palace wakes up, and for this reason we cannot get there; can you undertake to shoot it dead?"

"Yes," he said, "that will be a little bit of fun for me."

After this he got into a boat and rowed over the lake, and as soon as he landed, the little dog came running out, and was about to bark, but the huntsman took his air gun and shot it dead. When the giants saw that, they rejoiced, and thought they already had the King's daughter safe, but the huntsman wished first to see how matters stood, and told them that they must stay outside until he called them.

Then he went into the castle, and all was perfectly quiet within, and every one was asleep. When he opened the door of the first room, a sword was hanging on the wall which was made of pure silver, and there was a golden star on it, and the name of the King, and on a table near it lay a sealed letter which he broke open, and inside it was written that whosoever had the sword could kill everything which opposed him. So he took the sword from the wall, hung it at his side and went onwards: then he entered the room where the King's daughter was lying sleeping, and she was so beautiful that he stood still and, holding his breath, looked at her. He thought to himself, "How can I give an innocent maiden into the power of the wild giants, who have evil in their minds?"

He looked about further, and under the bed stood a pair of slippers, on the right one was her father's name with a star, and on the left her own name with a star. She wore also a great neckerchief of silk embroidered with gold, and on the right side was her father's name, and on the left her own, all in golden letters. Then the huntsman took a pair of scissors and cut the right corner off, and put it in his knapsack, and then he also took the right slipper with the King's name, and thrust that in.

Now the maiden still lay sleeping, and she was quite sewn into her nightdress, and he cut a morsel from this also, and thrust it in with the rest, but he did all without touching her. Then he went forth and left her lying asleep undisturbed, and when he came to the gate again, the giants were still standing outside waiting for him, and expecting that he was bringing the princess. But he cried to them that they were to come in, for the maiden was already in their power, that he could not open the gate to them, but there was a hole through which they must creep.

Then the first approached, and the huntsman wound the giant's hair around his hand, pulled the head in, and cut it off at one stroke with his sword, and then drew the rest of him in.

He called to the second and cut his head off likewise, and then he killed the third also, and he was well pleased that he had freed the beautiful maiden from her enemies, and he cut out their tongues and put them in his knapsack.

The Skillful Huntsman

Then he thought, "I will go home to my father and let him see what I have already done, and afterwards I will travel about the world; the luck which God is pleased to grant me will easily find me."

But when the King in the castle awoke, he saw the three giants lying there dead. So he went into the sleeping room of his daughter, awoke her, and asked who could have killed the giants?

Then she said, "Dear father, I know not, I have been asleep."

But when she arose and would have put on her slippers, the right one was gone, and when she looked at her neckerchief it was cut, and the right corner was missing, and when she looked at her nightdress a piece was cut out of it.

The King summoned his whole court together, soldiers and everyone else who was there, and asked who had set his daughter at liberty, and killed the giants?

Now it happened that he had a captain, who was one eyed and a hideous man, and he said that he had done it. Then the old King said that as he had accomplished this, he should marry his daughter.

But the maiden said, "Rather than marry him, dear father, I will go away into the world as far as my legs can carry me."

But the King said that if she would not marry him she should take off her royal garments and wear peasant's clothing, and go forth, and that she should go to a potter, and begin a trade in earthen vessels.

So she put off her royal apparel, and went to a potter and borrowed crockery enough for a stall, and she promised him also that if she had sold it by the evening, she would pay for it. Then the King said she was to seat herself in a corner with it and sell it, and he arranged with some peasants to drive over it with their carts, so that everything should be broken into a thousand pieces.

When therefore the King's daughter had placed her stall in the street, by came the carts, and broke all she had into tiny fragments. She began to weep and said, "Alas, how shall I ever pay for the pots now?"

The King had, however, wished by this to force her to marry the captain; but instead of that, she again went to the potter, and asked him if he would lend to her once more.

He said, "No," she must first pay for the things she had already had.

Then she went to her father and cried and lamented, and said she would go forth into the world.

Then he said, "I will have a little hut built for you in the forest outside, and in it you shall stay all your life long and cook for everyone, but you shall take no money for it."

When the hut was ready, a sign was hung on the door whereon was written, "Today given, tomorrow sold." There she remained a long time, and it was rumored about the world that a maiden was there who cooked without asking for payment, and that this was set forth on a sign outside her door.

The huntsman heard it likewise, and thought to himself, "That would suit you. You are poor, and have no money." So he took his air gun and his knapsack, wherein all the things which he had formerly carried away with him from the castle as tokens of his truthfulness were still lying, and went into the forest, and found the hut with the sign, "Today given, tomorrow sold."

He had put on the sword with which he had cut off the heads of the three giants, and then entered the hut, and ordered something to eat to be given to him. He was charmed with the beautiful maiden, who was indeed as lovely as any picture.

She asked him where he came and where he was going, and he said, "I am roaming about the world."

Then she asked him where he had got the sword, for that truly her father's name was on it. He asked her if she were the King's daughter.

"Yes," she answered.

"With this sword," he said, "did I cut off the heads of three giants." And he took their tongues out of his knapsack in proof. Then he also showed her the slipper, and the corner of the neckerchief, and the bit of the nightdress.

As a result, she was overjoyed, and said that he was the one who had delivered her. On this they went together to the old King, and fetched him to the hut, and she led him into her room, and told him that the huntsman was the man who had really set her free from the giants.

And when the aged King saw all the proofs of this, he could no longer doubt, and said that he was very glad he knew how everything had happened, and that the huntsman should have

The Skillful Huntsman

her to wife, on which the maiden was glad at heart.

Then she dressed the huntsman as if he were a foreign lord, and the King ordered a feast to be prepared. When they went to table, the captain sat on the left side of the King's daughter, but the huntsman was on the right, and the captain thought he was a foreign lord who had come on a visit. When they had eaten and drunk, the old King said to the captain that he would set before him something which he must guess. "Supposing anyone said that he had killed the three giants and he were asked where the giants' tongues were, and he were forced to go and look, and there were none in their heads, how could that happen?"

The captain said, "Then they cannot have had any."

"Not so," said the King. "Every animal has a tongue," and then he likewise asked what anyone would deserve who made such an answer?

The captain replied, "He ought to be torn in pieces."

Then the King said he had pronounced his own sentence, and the captain was put in prison and then torn in four pieces; but the King's daughter was married to the huntsman.

After this he brought his father and mother, and they lived with their son in happiness, and after the death of the old King he received the kingdom.

* * *

WE'RE not surprised to discover that the Grimm brothers tell story after story of princesses living *happily ever after* in wedded bliss. This is another such tale. But what makes it stand out from the others? What makes it different? The huntsman.

The story of a bridegroom and his bride always finds its origin in Christ and the Church. In this story we're shown a certain side of Christ, as displayed in the huntsman. Christ is a giant slayer. Yes, a giant slayer, armed and dangerous.

If you recall, when we looked at *The Giant and the Tailor* we discovered that the giant in that tale had attributes that describe God. Remember?

The Skillful Huntsman

> The giant is described as 'all powerful' (Luke 1:37; Job 11:7-11) and speaks with a voice as if it were thundering on every side' (Ex. 19:19). He says to the tailor, 'you may have a place with me' (Deut. 33:27; John 12:26; John 14:3). The giant is God!

In this tale the skillful huntsman shoots the meat of an ox (an animal offered in sacrifice to God – Deut. 17:1) out of a giant's mouth. Is this an allusion to the One True God depriving sustenance from the false gods of this world, removing the meat offerings from their hands, from their mouths?

The three giants (false gods) are deprived food as the huntsman (Christ) begins the process of destroying their wickedness altogether. Take note of how the Grimm's messianic figure attacks these giants. He uses his air gun. Air? Yes. An air gun with a special ability. It always hit its mark. The use of this air gun prompts the giant to say, "Well, really... if the *wind* has not blown the bit out of my hand!" (emphasis mine)

Air and wind. O, how clever our storytellers were. A huntsman and an air gun. Christ and the "sword of the Spirit" (Eph. 6:17).

The Greek word for *spirit* in Ephesians 6:17 carries with it meanings such as *wind* and *breath*. It's all about air. The Holy Spirit of God always hits the mark. The "air gun" of God doesn't miss (Is. 55:11).

The use of the air gun, a type of sword of the Spirit, leads to the huntsman using an actual sword. A sword that can kill everything that opposes its bearer. This sword, a further allusion to the Spirit, has upon it the word of the King, his name. "And take... the sword of the Spirit, which is the word of God..." (Eph. 6:17)

Air and a word-bearing sword. It's all right there, craftily implanted into a fairy tale that is captivating and engaging in its own right, but with a connection to truth for those who have eyes to see and ears to hear.

With this sword the huntsman cuts off the head of the "wild giants, who [had] evil in their minds." Or in other words, the false gods.

> He was well pleased that he had freed the beautiful maiden [the Church] from her enemies [false gods], and he cut out their tongues and put them in his knapsack. Then he thought, 'I will go home to my

The Skillful Huntsman

father and let him see what I have already done, and afterwards I will travel about the world.

Not only has Christ defeated the false gods of this world, the devil and his demons, but He has also made them mute. He cut out their tongues on the cross, and then went home to His Father in heaven, from where He will come again to be with His people in the new heaven and the new earth (Rev. 21:1). For as Scripture says, "the dwelling place of God is with man" (Rev. 21:3).

Does this mean that evil won't still impact us in the days before our Lord returns? No. Liars will rise up and try to claim the feats of Christ as their own. Antichrist's will deceive and attempt to take for themselves the bride who belongs to Jesus, just as the King's captain lied and tried to wed the maiden whose hand rightfully belonged to the huntsman.

However, these antichrist's will meet an end similar to the false gods (giants). They'll be destroyed. Ironically, their tongues will speak the very words of their death sentence, for their deceitful mouths are what give voice and the appearance of life to the evil of the silenced and dead giants (false gods).

Allerleirauh

THERE was once on a time a King who had a wife with golden hair, and she was so beautiful that her equal was not to be found on earth. It came to pass that she lay ill, and as she felt that she must soon die, she called the King and said, "If you wish to marry again after my death, take no one who is not quite as beautiful as I am, and who has not just such golden hair as I have: this you must promise me." And after the King had promised her this she closed her eyes and died.

For a long time the King could not be comforted, and had no thought of taking another wife. At length his councilors said, "There is no help for it, the King must marry again, that we may have a Queen." And now messengers were sent about far and wide, to seek a bride who equaled the late Queen in beauty. In the whole world, however, none was to be found, and even if one had been found, still there would have been no one who had such golden hair. So the messengers came home as they went.

Now the King had a daughter, who was just as beautiful as her dead mother, and had the same golden hair. When she was grown up the King looked at her one day, and saw that in every respect she was like his late wife, and suddenly felt a violent love for her. Then he spoke to his councilors, "I will marry my daughter, for she is the counterpart of my late wife, otherwise I can find no bride who resembles her."

When the councilors heard that, they were shocked, and said, "God has forbidden a father to marry his daughter, no good can come from such a crime, and the kingdom will be involved in the ruin."

The daughter was still more shocked when she became aware of her father's resolution, but hoped to turn him from his design. Then she said to him, "Before I fulfill your wish, I must have three dresses, one as golden as the sun, one as silvery as the moon, and one as bright as the stars; besides this, I wish for a mantle of a thousand different kinds of fur and hair joined together, and one of every kind of animal in your kingdom must give a piece of his skin for it." But she thought, "To get that will be quite impossible, and therefore I shall divert my father from his wicked intentions."

The King, however, did not give it up, and the cleverest maidens in his kingdom had to weave the three dresses, one as golden as the sun, one as silvery as the moon, and one as bright as the stars, and his huntsmen had to catch one of every kind of animal in the whole of his kingdom, and take from it a piece of its skin, and out of these was made a mantle of a thousand different kinds of fur.

At length, when all was ready, the King caused the mantle to be brought, spread it out before her, and said, "The wedding shall be tomorrow."

When, therefore, the King's daughter saw that there was no longer any hope of turning her father's heart, she resolved to run away from him. In the night while everyone was asleep, she got up, and took three different things from her treasures, a golden ring, a golden spinning wheel, and a golden reel. The three dresses of the sun, moon, and stars she put into a nutshell, put on her mantle of all kinds of fur, and blackened her face and hands with soot. Then she commended herself to God, and went away, and walked the whole night until she reached a great forest. And as she was tired, she got into a hollow tree, and fell asleep. The sun rose, and she slept on, and she was still sleeping when it was full day.

Then it so happened that the King to whom this forest belonged, was hunting in it. When his dogs came to the tree, they sniffed, and ran barking around about it. The King said to the huntsmen, "Just see what kind of wild beast has hidden itself in there."

The huntsmen obeyed his order, and when they came back they said, "A wondrous beast is lying in the hollow tree; we have never before seen one like it. Its skin is fur of a thousand different kinds, but it is lying asleep."

The King said, "See if you can catch it alive, and then fasten it to the carriage, and we will take it with us."

When the huntsmen laid hold of the maiden, she awoke full of terror, and cried to them, "I am a poor child, deserted by father and mother; have pity on me, and take me with you."

Then they said, "Allerleirauh, you will be useful in the kitchen, come with us, and you can sweep up the ashes." So they put her in the carriage, and took her home to the royal palace. There they pointed out to her a closet under the stairs, where no daylight entered, and said, "Hairy animal, there you can live and sleep."

Then she was sent into the kitchen, and there she carried wood and water, swept the hearth, plucked the fowls, picked the vegetables, raked the ashes, and did all the dirty work.

Allerleirauh lived there for a long time in great wretchedness. Alas, fair princess, what is to become of thee now!

It happened, however, that one day a feast was held in the palace, and she said to the cook, "May I go upstairs for a while, and look on? I will place myself outside the door."

The cook answered, "Yes, go, but you must be back here in half-an-hour to sweep the hearth."

Then she took her oil lamp, went into her den, put off her fur dress, and washed the soot off her face and hands, so that her full beauty once more came to light. And she opened the nut, and took out her dress which shone like the sun, and when she had done that she went up to the festival, and every one made way for her, for no one knew her, and thought no otherwise than that she was a king's daughter.

The King came to meet her, gave his hand to her, and danced with her, and thought in his heart, "My eyes have never yet seen any one so beautiful!" When the dance was over she curtsied, and when the King looked around again she had vanished, and none knew where. The guards who stood outside the palace were called and questioned, but no one had seen her.

She had, however, run into her little den, had quickly taken off her dress, made her face and hands black again, put on the fur mantle, and again was Allerleirauh. And now when she went into the kitchen, and was about to get to her work and sweep up the ashes, the cook said, "Leave that alone till morning, and make me the soup for the King; I, too, will go upstairs awhile, and take a look; but let no hairs fall in, or in future you shall have nothing to eat."

So the cook went away, and Allerleirauh made the soup for the king, and made bread soup and the best she could, and when it was ready she fetched her golden ring from her little den, and put it in the bowl in which the soup was served. When the dancing was over, the King had his soup brought and ate it, and he liked it so much that it seemed to him he had never tasted better. But when he came to the bottom of the bowl, he saw a golden ring lying, and could not conceive how it could have got there. Then he ordered the cook to appear before him.

The cook was terrified when he heard the order, and said to Allerleirauh, "You have certainly let a hair fall into the soup, and if you have, you shall be beaten for it." When he came before the King the latter asked who had made the soup?

The cook replied, "I made it."

But the King said, "That is not true, for it was much better than usual, and cooked differently."

He answered, "I must acknowledge that I did not make it, it was made by the rough animal."

The King said, "Go and bid it come up here."

When Allerleirauh came, the King said, "Who are you?"

"I am a poor girl who no longer has any father or mother."

He asked further, "Of what use are you in my palace?"

She answered, "I am good for nothing but to have boots thrown at my head."

He continued, "Where did you get the ring which was in the soup?"

She answered, "I know nothing about the ring."

So the King could learn nothing, and had to send her away again.

After a while, there was another festival, and then, as before, Allerleirauh begged the cook for leave to go and look on.

He answered, "Yes, but come back again in half-an-hour, and make the King the bread soup which he so much likes."

Then she ran into her den, washed herself quickly, and took out of the nut the dress which was as silvery as the moon, and put it on. Then she went up and was like a princess, and the King stepped forward to meet her, and rejoiced to see her once more, and as the dance was just beginning they danced it together. But when it was ended, she again disappeared so quickly that the King could not observe where she

Allerleirauh

went. She, however, sprang into her den, and once more made herself a hairy animal, and went into the kitchen to prepare the bread soup.

When the cook had gone up-stairs, she fetched the little golden spinning wheel, and put it in the bowl so that the soup covered it. Then it was taken to the King, who ate it, and liked it as much as before, and had the cook brought, who this time likewise was forced to confess that Allerleirauh had prepared the soup. Allerleirauh again came before the King, but she answered that she was good for nothing else but to have boots thrown at her head, and that she knew nothing at all about the little golden spinning wheel.

When, for the third time, the King held a festival, all happened just as it had done before.

The cook said, "Faith rough-skin, you are a witch, and always put something in the soup which makes it so good that the King likes it better than that which I cook," but as she begged so hard, he let her go up at the appointed time. And now she put on the dress which shone like the stars, and thus entered the hall.

Again the King danced with the beautiful maiden, and thought that she never yet had been so beautiful. And while she was dancing, he contrived, without her noticing it, to slip a golden ring on her finger, and he had given orders that the dance should last a very long time. When it was ended, he wanted to hold her fast by her hands, but she tore herself loose, and sprang away so quickly through the crowd that she vanished from his sight. She ran as fast as she could into her den beneath the stairs, but as she had been too long, and had stayed more than half-an-hour she could not take off her pretty dress, but only threw over it her fur mantle, and in her haste she did not make herself quite black, but one finger remained white.

Then Allerleirauh ran into the kitchen, and cooked the bread soup for the King, and as the cook was away, put her golden reel into it. When the King found the reel at the bottom of it, he caused Allerleirauh to be summoned, and then he spied the white finger, and saw the ring which he had put on it during the dance. Then he grasped her by the hand, and held her fast, and when she wanted to release herself and run away, her mantle of fur opened a little, and the

Allerleirauh

star dress shone forth. The King clutched the mantle and tore it off. Then her golden hair shone forth, and she stood there in full splendor, and could no longer hide herself. And when she had washed the soot and ashes from her face, she was more beautiful than anyone who had ever been seen on earth.

But the King said, "You are my dear bride, and we will never more part from each other." After that the marriage was solemnized, and they lived happily until their death.

* * *

IF we wish to venture any further into the wondrous world of fairyland, we would be wise to prepare ourselves for the abundance of princess stories that occupy the fortified castles and fairy-filled forests we will encounter. The volume with which they occur is itself a fascinating fact for the reader on a quest to find God's truth in the stories of man. The Bridegroom comes to rescue His bride. It's a theme that would appear to predominate fairyland, if not all the corridors of fiction that fill our libraries.

If the central event in human history is the incarnation of Christ – the Bridegroom rescuing the Church – it makes sense that mankind would repeat this theme in story after story, intentionally or otherwise.

But what does that mean for you and me? Are we to close our books and conclude that that is all there is to every story? By no means. Did not four men record the Gospel of our Lord? And even within just the synoptics, are there not nuances and distinctions that teach us truth? Indeed, there are.

We find a unique expression of the truth with each fairy tale, and yes, with each princess we meet. So, what do we find in the story of Allerleirauh?

The answer is in the title, which is the princess' name, Allerleirauh. This German word translated into English means "All kinds of fur." When we focus our attention there we see that this story presents the relationship between the Old Testament's sacrificial system and the sacrifice of Christ on the cross.

There is a great wickedness in the beginning of the story – a father who wishes to marry his own daughter.

Allerleirauh

> When the councilors heard [that the king wished to marry his daughter] they were shocked, and said, "God has forbidden a father to marry his daughter, no good can come from such a crime, and the kingdom will be involved in the ruin."

The fairyland counselors have a clear understanding of God's Law. Everyone would suffer the ruin the sin would bring about. We're pleased to read that the King's daughter develops a plan to free the kingdom from the sin and suffering.

> Before I fulfill your wish, I must have three dresses, one as golden as the sun, one as silvery as the moon, and one as bright as the stars; besides this, I wish for a mantle of a thousand different kinds of fur and hair joined together, and one of every kind of animal in your kingdom must give a piece of his skin for it.

Consider the second half of her demand. She wants a garment made of every kind of animal in the kingdom. That's a lot of dead animals. For what purpose? To "divert [her] father from his wicked intentions." To deal with sin. The Old Testament sacrificial system involved a lot of dead animals, and for the same reason, to cover the sins of the people.

The princess's father didn't give up; he continued in his sin. The three dresses were made, as was the mantle of a thousand different furs. He persisted in his wickedness. The shedding of blood that had, to that point, worked against the sin would either be all for naught or would lead to the actual means by which sin is undone, the source of its effectiveness – the final sacrifice. Of course, I'm speaking of the death of Christ.[23]

In Allerleirauh, like in the Old Testament, the sacrifice of animals for the benefit of the kingdom (Israel) wasn't wholly sufficient. The sacrifices are a precursor to the ultimate sacrifice of the Lamb of God, who takes away the sin of the world (John 1:29). In our fairytale, the making of the mantle is much the same. The princess' plan, though it was insufficient in staying the sin of her father, was the precursor to a new life, for her and consequently for her father's kingdom that was

---

[23] Read Hebrews 10 to further grasp the relationship between Christ and the sacrifices of the Old Testament.

Allerleirauh

freed from his sinful desires once she was gone. This new life came only after an episode with a tree.

Yes, the hollow tree in which our princess sleeps, covered in a thousand different kinds of fur, draws our imagination to the tree of Christ, the place where the sacrifices of the Old Testament terminate, the cross, the place where Jesus said, "It is finished" (John 19:30), where full atonement was made for the ruinous sins of mankind.

This point is underscored in that she is covered in what is described as a "fur of a thousand different kinds." In Scripture the number 1000 symbolizes completion and perfection. The cross is where the imperfect animal sacrifices find their perfection. The cross is also where we see "a wondrous beast," so to speak, that "we have never before seen," namely a perfect human being, Jesus Christ.

What follows in our tale is the threefold revelation of our beautiful princess. Should we be surprised that this takes place when she "washed the soot off of her face and hands, so that her full beauty once more came to light"? Not at all. It's baptism! After which "she went up to the festival."

The Grimm brothers spread this out across three episodes that give opportunity to display the princess's humble heart as she is hidden under a thousand furs and declares, "I am good for nothing but to have boots thrown at my head."

In baptism the Christian is hidden in the humility of Christ, covered in the mantle of His perfect and complete sacrifice, His robe of righteousness (Is. 61:10). But this hiddenness is not permanent. Consider Colossians 3:1-3.

> If then you have been raised with Christ, seek the things that are above, where Christ is, seated at the right hand of God. Set your minds on things that are above, not on things that are on earth. For you have died, and your life is hidden with Christ in God. When Christ who is your life appears, then you also will appear with him in glory.

Is that not what is being conveyed at the end of our tale?

> The King clutched the mantle and tore it off. Then her golden hair shone forth, and

she stood there in full splendor, and could no longer hide herself. And when she had washed the soot and ashes from her face, she was more beautiful than anyone who had ever been seen on earth.

But the King said, 'You are my dear bride, and we will never more part from each other.' After that the marriage was solemnized, and they lived happily ever after until their death.

Cinderella

THE wife of a rich man fell sick, and as she felt that her end was drawing near, she called her only daughter to her bedside and said, "Dear child, be good and pious, and then the good God will always protect you, and I will look down on you from heaven and be near you." After that she closed her eyes and departed.

Every day the maiden went out to her mother's grave, and wept, and she remained pious and good. When winter came the snow spread a white sheet over the grave, and when the spring sun had drawn it off again, the man had taken another wife.

The woman had brought two daughters into the house with her, who were beautiful

Cinderella

and fair of face, but vile and black of heart. Now began a bad time for the poor step-child.

"Is the stupid goose to sit in the parlor with us?" they said. "He who wants to eat bread must earn it; out with the kitchen wench."

They took her pretty clothes away from her, put an old grey bed gown on her, and gave her wooden shoes.

"Just look at the proud princess, how decked out she is!" they cried, and laughed, and led her into the kitchen.

There she had to do hard work from morning till night, get up before daybreak, carry water, light fires, cook and wash. Besides this, the sisters did her every imaginable injury – they mocked her and emptied her peas and lentils into the ashes, so that she was forced to sit and pick them out again. In the evening when she had worked till she was weary she had no bed to go to, but had to sleep by the fireside in the ashes. And as on that account she always looked dusty and dirty, they called her Cinderella.

It happened that the father was once going to the fair, and he asked his two step-daughters what he should bring back for them.

"Beautiful dresses," said one.

"Pearls and jewels," said the second.

"And you, Cinderella," he said, "what will you have?"

"Father, break off for me the first branch which knocks against your hat on your way home."

So he bought beautiful dresses, pearls and jewels for his two step-daughters, and on his way home, as he was riding through a green thicket, a hazel twig brushed against him and knocked off his hat. Then he broke off the branch and took it with him. When he reached home he gave his step-daughters the things which they had wished for, and to Cinderella he gave the branch from the hazel-bush.

Cinderella thanked him, went to her mother's grave and planted the branch on it, and wept so much that the tears fell down on it and watered it. And it grew, however, and became a handsome tree. Three times a day Cinderella went and sat beneath it, and wept and prayed, and a little white bird always came on the tree, and if Cinderella expressed a wish, the bird threw down to her what she had wished for.

It happened, however, that the King appointed a festival which was to last three days, and to which all the beautiful young girls in the country were invited, in order that his son might choose himself a bride. When the two step-sisters heard that they too were to appear among the number, they were delighted, called Cinderella and said, "Comb our hair for us, brush our shoes and fasten our buckles, for we are going to the festival at the King's palace."

Cinderella obeyed, but wept, because she too would have liked to go with them to the dance, and begged her step-mother to allow her to do so.

"You go, Cinderella!" she said; "You are dusty and dirty and would go to the festival? You have no clothes and shoes, and yet would dance!"

As, however, Cinderella went on asking, the step-mother at last said, "I have emptied a dish of lentils into the ashes for you, if you have picked them out again in two hours, you shall go with us."

The maiden went through the backdoor into the garden, and called,

> *"You tame pigeons, you turtle doves,*
> *and all you birds beneath the sky,*

> *come and help me to pick*
> *The good into the pot,*
> *The bad into the crop."*

Then two white pigeons came in by the kitchen window, and afterwards the turtle doves, and at last all the birds beneath the sky, came whirring and crowding in, and alighted amongst the ashes. And the pigeons nodded with their heads and began pick, pick, pick, pick, and the rest began also pick, pick, pick, pick, and gathered all the good grains into the dish. Hardly had one hour passed before they had finished, and all flew out again.

Then the girl took the dish to her step-mother, and was glad, and believed that now she would be allowed to go with them to the festival.

But the step-mother said, "No, Cinderella, you have no clothes and you cannot dance; you would only be laughed at." And as Cinderella wept at this, the step-mother said, "If you can pick two dishes of lentils out of the ashes for me in one hour, you shall go with us." And she thought to herself, "That she most certainly cannot do."

When the step-mother had emptied the two dishes of lentils amongst the ashes, the maiden went through the backdoor into the garden and cried,

> *"You tame pigeons, you turtle-doves,*
> *and all you birds beneath the sky,*
> *come and help me to pick*
>   *The good into the pot,*
>   *The bad into the crop."*

Then two white pigeons came in by the kitchen window, and afterwards the turtle doves, and at length all the birds beneath the sky, came whirring and crowding in, and alighted amongst the ashes. And the doves nodded with their heads and began pick, pick, pick, pick, and the others began also pick, pick, pick, pick, and gathered all the good seeds into the dishes, and before half an hour was over they had already finished, and all flew out again. Then the maiden carried the dishes to the step-mother and was delighted, and believed that she might now go with them to the festival.

But the step-mother said, "All this will not help you; you cannot go with us, for you have no clothes and cannot dance; we should be ashamed of you!" On this she turned her back on Cinderella, and hurried away with her two proud daughters.

As no one was now at home, Cinderella went to her mother's grave beneath the hazel tree, and cried,

> *"Shiver and quiver, little tree,*
> *Silver and gold throw down over me."*

Then the bird threw a gold and silver dress down to her, and slippers embroidered with silk and silver.

She put on the dress with all speed, and went to the festival. Her step-sisters and the step-mother however did not know her, and thought she must be a foreign princess, for she looked so beautiful in the golden dress. They never once thought of Cinderella, and believed that she was sitting at home in the dirt, picking lentils out of the ashes.

The prince went to meet her, took her by the hand and danced with her. He would dance with no other maiden, and never left loose of her hand, and if anyone else came to invite her, he said, "This is my partner."

She danced till it was evening, and then she wanted to go home. But the King's son said, "I will go with you and keep you company," for he wished to see to whom the beautiful maiden belonged. She escaped from him, however, and sprang into the pigeon-house.

The King's son waited until her father came, and then he told him that the stranger maiden had leapt into the pigeon house. The old man thought, "Can it be Cinderella?" and they had to bring him an axe and a pickaxe that he might hew the pigeon house to pieces, but no one was inside it. And when they got home Cinderella lay in her dirty clothes among the ashes, and a dim little oil lamp was burning on the mantle-piece, for Cinderella had jumped quickly down from the back of the pigeon house and had run to the little hazel tree, and there she had taken off her beautiful clothes and laid them on the grave, and the bird had taken them away again, and then she had placed herself in the kitchen amongst the ashes in her grey gown.

The next day when the festival began afresh, and her parents and the step-sisters had gone once more, Cinderella went to the hazel tree and said—

*"Shiver and quiver, little tree,
Silver and gold throw down over me."*

Then the bird threw down a much more beautiful dress than on the preceding day. And when Cinderella appeared at the festival in this dress, everyone was astonished at her beauty.

The King's son had waited until she came, and instantly took her by the hand and danced with no one but her. When others came and invited her, he said, "She is my partner."

When evening came she wished to leave, and the King's son followed her and wanted to see into which house she went. But she sprang away from him, and into the garden behind the house. Therein stood a beautiful tall tree on which hung the most magnificent pears. She clambered so nimbly between the branches like a squirrel that the King's son did not know where she was gone.

He waited until her father came, and said to him, "The stranger maiden has escaped from me, and I believe she has climbed up the pear tree."

The father thought, "Can it be Cinderella?" and had an axe brought and cut the tree down, but no one was on it. And when they got into the kitchen, Cinderella lay there amongst the ashes, as usual, for she had jumped down on the other side of the tree, had taken the beautiful dress to the bird on the little hazel tree, and put on her grey gown.

On the third day, when the parents and sisters had gone away, Cinderella went once more to her mother's grave and said to the little tree,—

"Shiver and quiver, little tree,
Silver and gold throw down over me."

And now the bird threw down to her a dress which was more splendid and magnificent than any she had yet had, and the slippers were golden.

And when she went to the festival in the dress, no one knew how to speak for astonishment. The King's son danced with her only, and if any one invited her to dance, he said, "She is my partner."

When evening came, Cinderella wished to leave, and the King's son was anxious to go with her, but she escaped from him so quickly that he could not follow her. The King's son had, however, used a stratagem, and had caused the whole staircase to be smeared with pitch, and there, when she ran down, had the maiden's left slipper remained sticking. The King's son picked it up, and it was small and dainty, and all golden.

The next morning, he went with it to the father, and said to him, "No one shall be my wife but she whose foot this golden slipper fits."

Then were the two sisters glad, for they had pretty feet. The eldest went with the shoe into her room and wanted to try it on, and her mother stood by. But she could not get her big toe into it, and the shoe was too small for her.

Then her mother gave her a knife and said, "Cut the toe off; when you are Queen you will have no more need to go on foot."

The maiden cut the toe off, forced the foot into the shoe, swallowed the pain, and went out to the King's son.

Then he took her on his horse as his bride and rode away with her. They were, however, obliged to pass the grave, and there, on the hazel tree, sat the two pigeons and cried,

"Turn and peep, turn and peep,

*There's blood within the shoe,
The shoe it is too small for her,
The true bride waits for you."*

Then he looked at her foot and saw how the blood was streaming from it. He turned his horse around and took the false bride home again, and said she was not the true one, and that the other sister was to put the shoe on.

Then this one went into her chamber and got her toes safely into the shoe, but her heel was too large. So her mother gave her a knife and said, "Cut a bit off thy heel; when you are Queen you will have no more need to go on foot."

The maiden cut a bit off her heel, forced her foot into the shoe, swallowed the pain, and went out to the King's son. He took her on his horse as his bride, and rode away with her, but when they passed by the hazel tree, two little pigeons sat on it and cried,

*"Turn and peep, turn and peep,
There's blood within the shoe
The shoe it is too small for her,
The true bride waits for you."*

He looked down at her foot and saw how the blood was running out of her shoe, and how it had stained her white stocking. Then he turned his horse and took the false bride home again. "This also is not the right one," he said, "have you no other daughter?"

"No," said the man, "There is still a little stunted kitchen wench which my late wife left behind her, but she cannot possibly be the bride."

The King's son said he was to send her up to him; but the mother answered, "Oh, no, she is much too dirty, she cannot show herself!" He absolutely insisted on it, and Cinderella had to be called.

She first washed her hands and face clean, and then went and bowed down before the King's son, who gave her the golden shoe. Then she seated herself on a stool, drew her foot out of the heavy wooden shoe, and put it into the slipper, which fit like a glove. And when she rose up and the King's son looked at her face he recognized the beautiful maiden who had danced with him and cried, "That is the true bride!"

The step-mother and the two sisters were terrified and became pale with rage; he, however, took Cinderella on his horse and rode away with her. As they passed by the hazel tree, the two white doves cried,

> *"Turn and peep, turn and peep,*
> *No blood is in the shoe,*
> *The shoe is not too small for her,*
> *The true bride rides with you,"*

and when they had cried that, the two came flying down and placed themselves on Cinderella's shoulders, one on the right, the other on the left, and remained sitting there.

When the wedding with the King's son had to be celebrated, the two false sisters came and wanted to get into favor with Cinderella and share her good fortune. When the betrothed couple went to church, the elder was at the right side and the younger at the left, and the pigeons pecked out one eye of each of them. Afterwards as they came back, the elder was at the left, and the younger at the right, and then the pigeons pecked out the other eye of each. Therefore, for their wickedness and falsehood, they were punished with blindness as long as they lived.

* * *

FOR many this is the most beloved fairy tale in the Grimm brothers' collection. A familiar story that continues to inspire little girls to dream of faraway castles and happy endings. Thanks to Walt Disney's popularized depiction of the mourning maiden, merely mention the name Cinderella and a princess with blonde hair and a blue dress twirls to life in one's imagination. The princess of princesses she is.

It's clear from the story that living in fairy land is no different from living in the real world, at least with respect to our fall into sin. Death casts a broad shadow. But in the face of death a promise was given, both in Scripture and in the Cinderella story, a promise of communion, of hope and protection—salvation.

In Scripture salvation in Jesus Christ is the promise given immediately after death became a reality. We find it in Genesis 3:15: the first Gospel message, what the Church calls the *protoevangelion*. It's the declaration that God will save us, that He will never abandon us. It tells how we're brought into communion with Him through the death of woman's offspring –

Jesus—and given hope in the resurrection, death's defeat.

In our fairy tale this Gospel message is also delivered to a woman's offspring, the only daughter of a dying mother: "Dear child, be good and pious, and then the good God will always protect you, and I will look down on you from heaven and be near you."

One might find further hints of the crucifixion in what immediately follows in the story. The girl's father remarries and two stepdaughters arrive on the scene. It's not, however, by either of these two that we're given our happy ending. It's not by the two thieves on the left and right of the Messiah that we have salvation, but only by the death and resurrection of the good and pious Jesus. When these two "vile and black of heart" step-sisters enter the picture (who by the end of the story try their hand at thievery), a bad time began "for the poor step-child," the one who didn't belong among them.

The Christian reader may detect, here at the beginning of the story, that these two sisters are multifaceted fill-ins. The Sandhedrin and the Roman soldiers had roles in the crucifixion of Christ. In addition to representing the thieves atop Calvary, the sisters also play these two other parts. First, like the Sanhedrin, they show their ignorance of Scripture. Next, in a fashion reminiscent of the Roman soldiers, they take away her clothes, replacing them with different attire (Matt. 27:27-31). The Sanhedrin didn't understand what God revealed in what we refer to as the Old Testament. For the step-sisters it's a New Testament passage, 2 Thessalonians 3:10, that is misunderstood. Imagining them among the soldiers mocking Jesus isn't the least bit difficult.

Why the 2 Thessalonians passage? They're implying that Cinderella is a freeloader, and in her own father's house! 2 Thessalonians deals with entitlement, breaking with tradition, serving neighbor, and not being a burden on others. Even the most casual reader is able to determine who in the story is busy and who are the busybodies (2 Thess. 3:11). When it comes to the step-sisters' accusation that Cinderella is not earning her keep, well, it's clear that the shoe is on the other foot, er, feet. The shoe that fits Cinderella is a different one, one of piety and goodness, and she wears it gracefully.

There is much to discuss in this tale, but let's focus on just one thing more, worship. The grave of Cinderella's mother became a place of worship for the girl. She planted a branch that grew into a handsome tree from the torrent of tears she wept there. Similar to Eden and the tree of the knowledge of good and evil, where God came to Adam and Eve in His Word of prohibition, the place of death became the place that fostered her faith and gave Cinderella strength. The place of Christ's death—the cross—became the tree that sustains Christian faith, the place where God's good Word conquered evil forever.

> Three times a day Cinderella went and sat beneath it, and wept and prayed, and a little white bird [think dove, think Holy Spirit] always came on the tree, and if Cinderella expressed a wish, the bird threw down to her what she had wished for.

"Ask, and it will be given to you." (Matt. 7:7. See also Luke 11:9; Mark 11:24; Ps. 37:4; Is. 30:19; Matt. 21:22). Cinderella had faith. She asked and it was given. Her faith is what carries this tale forward. She relied on

God, the bird, as she spoke (in prayer) to the little tree—a beautiful portrayal of the Christian turning to Christ who hung in humility upon the tree of the cross. Through the cross of Christ God provides us what we need, He answers all prayers upon it's bloodied branches. Likewise, the bird (God) provides Cinderella with what she needs at the graveside tree. He gives and He takes away (Job 1:21) as it benefits the child of faith.

Cinderella is the story of the Christian and how our Lord works all things for our benefit (Rom. 8:28). We come to church where we're brought into communion with God, where we receive the fruit of the tree of the cross, where we're sustained, our lives carried forward. It all happens at the tree, the place where God comes to the believer as was promised, the place where Christ bloodied his feet to give us life in the kingdom. His feet bled so ours wouldn't have to.

It's at the tree that false brides—liars—are made known. People will try to masquerade as the true bride of Christ, the Church, they may deceive man, but unbelievers cannot fool God. He sees that they're trying to enter the kingdom by way of their own blood—by what they've done—instead of by what He's done. This is all wrong. Christ's blood makes our slipper gold, whereas if we rely on our blood it stains the riches we've been given.

The points of comparison continue. But as I've gone on long enough, I trust you'll find them for yourself.

Acknowledgments

THANK you Jessica. You're always the first person to read my words. Your comments and suggestions never fail to improve my work.

Josh and Kasandra Radke, thank you for supporting this project and, Josh, for improving it with your editing skills. Thank you, Sam, for so generously agreeing to write the foreword and for the kind words offered therein.

Thank you to all who read the book prior to publication, and finally, thank you, dear reader, for setting out to find the Truth of God's Word in these twenty-five stories. I pray it has proven to be a blessing to you.

Tyrel Bramwell lives with his wife and children in Ferndale, California where he is the pastor of St. Mark's Evangelical Lutheran Church. He is also the author of *The Gift and the Defender*. His writing aims to enrich readers with a worldview that is packed with imagination, yet rooted in the knowable and absolute Truth of the Triune God. He has a bachelor's degree from Concordia University, Michigan and his master of divinity degree from Concordia Theological Seminary, Indiana.

Visit him online at moragunfighter.com

Made in the USA
Columbia, SC
02 November 2017